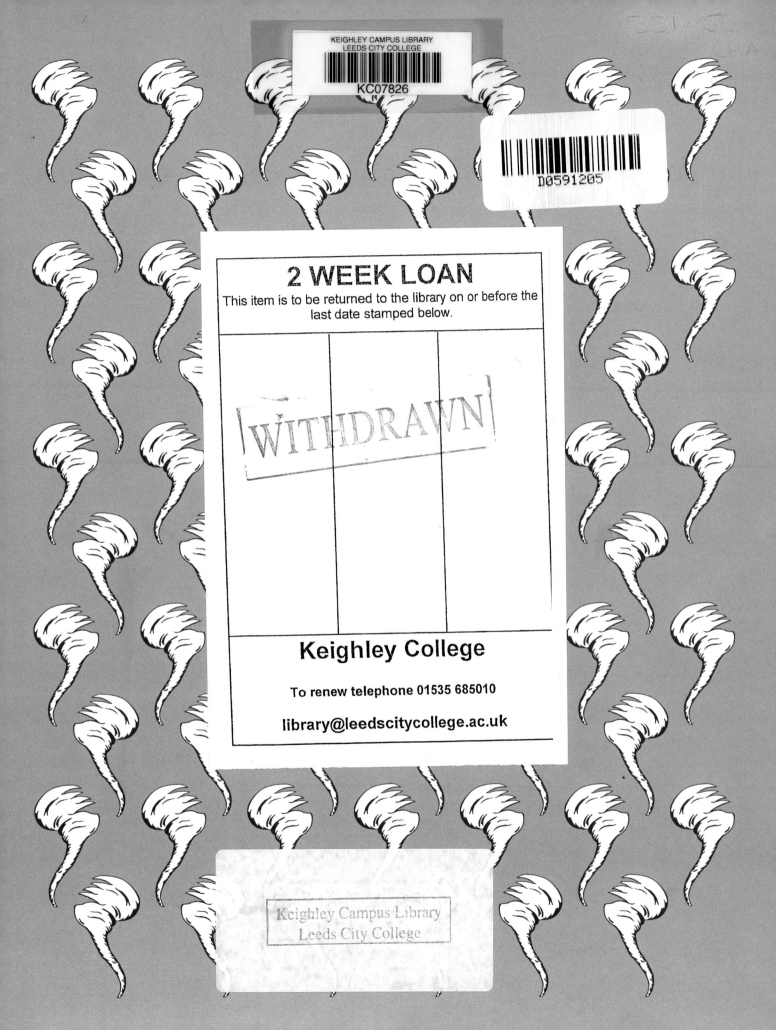

# 2 WEEK LOAN

This item is to be returned to the library on or before the last date stamped below.

WITHDRAWN

## Keighley College

**To renew telephone 01535 685010**

**library@leedscitycollege.ac.uk**

# HURRICANE
# & TORNADO

Cyclone shelter

Spots on the sun

Sunset at Stonehenge, England

19th-century
reproduction of Galileo's
original thermoscope

High-speed
winds encircle Saturn

Lighthouse at the
George Washington
Bridge in New
York, USA

Wind-eroded rocks
in Utah, USA

Ice
crystal

Pine cone
with open
scales
indicating
dry
weather

# DK EYEWITNESS GUIDES

# HURRICANE
# & TORNADO

Written by
## JACK CHALLONER

Simultaneous waterspout and lightning bolt

## Dorling Kindersley

Doppler-radar dome

Avalanche-warning sign

**Dorling Kindersley**
LONDON, NEW YORK, AUCKLAND, DELHI,
JOHANNESBURG, MUNICH, PARIS, and SYDNEY

For a full catalogue, visit

DK www.dk.com

**Project editor** Melanie Halton
**Art editor** Ann Cannings
**Managing editor** Sue Grabham
**Senior managing art editor** Julia Harris
**Editorial consultant** Lesley Newson
**Picture research** Mollie Gillard, Samantha Nunn
**DTP designers** Andrew O'Brien, Georgia Bryer
**Jacket designer** Margherita Gianni
**Production** Kate Oliver

This Eyewitness ® Guide has been conceived by
Dorling Kindersley Limited and Editions Gallimard

First published in Great Britain in 2000
by Dorling Kindersley Limited,
9 Henrietta Street, London WC2E 8PS

Copyright © 2000 Dorling Kindersley Limited, London

A CIP catalogue record for this book is
available from the British Library.

ISBN 0 7513 6216 6

Colour reproduction by Colourscan, Singapore
Printed in China by Toppan Printing Co. (Shenzhen) Ltd.

Venetian
blind twisted
by a tornado

Italian
thermometer
(1657)

Storm
system
on Earth
viewed
from space

Hurricane-
warning flags

Storm erupts
on the sun

# Contents

Icicle formation in Arizona, USA

# Weather folklore

IN ANCIENT TIMES, people had very little idea how the weather worked. Some realized that clouds were made of water, but they could not work out where the wind came from, and did not understand the sun. Many believed that the gods made the weather, so weather mythology is often associated with religion. Others relied on guesses based on simple observations of plants, animals, or the sky to make forecasts. Ideas and observations were handed down from generation to generation, as sayings or stories, and some are quite reliable. But only when we understand fully how the weather works can we predict it with any accuracy. Weather science began in ancient Greece, when philosophers tried to explain what caused the weather. Some of their ideas were correct, but they did not test their theories, so they were often wrong.

**CONE WATCH**
No one knows when people first noticed that pine cones open their scales in dry air and close them when the air is humid. But because the air normally becomes more humid before rainfall, pine cones can be used to forecast wet weather.

**PHENOMENAL THINKERS**
Philosophers Aristotle and Plato were among the first people to try to explain scientifically how the weather works. They lived about 2,400 years ago in ancient Greece, and wrote about cloud, hail, storm, and snow formation, and more unusual phenomena, such as sun haloes. Their ideas were very influential and were not challenged until about 2,000 years later.

Detail from an Italian fresco showing Plato and Aristotle (1511)

**CRY FOR RAIN**
These Yali tribesmen of New Guinea are performing a dance to call for rain. Without rain there will be no harvest. During part of this ritual, dancers carry grass, which is believed to pierce the eye of the sun, making it cry tears of rain.

**ANIMAL FORECASTS**
Many animals respond to changes in temperature, humidity, or atmospheric pressure. Cocks, for example, often crow, and mistlethrushes sing, just before a thunderstorm. Observing animal behaviour can therefore be a useful way of making weather forecasts.

## SUN WORSHIP
Since the beginning of recorded history, many cultures have worshipped the sun. Stonehenge, in England, is one of many ancient sites thought to have been a place of sun worship. Some of the stones line up to the point where the sun rises on the summer solstice (the day the sun is at its highest in the sky).

*Stonehenge was built between 2500 BC and 1500 BC*

## WATCHING THE SKY
An ancient Maori myth describes how the god of thunder and lightning, Tawhaki, went up to the sky disguised as a kite. Maori priests believed they could predict the weather by watching how kites, which they flew in Tawhaki's honour, moved across the sky.

*Maori kite made of canvas and twigs*

## MAGIC CHARMS
This figurehead from the Solomon Islands would have been attached to the front of a canoe to ward off dangerous storms at sea. Many lucky charms, used by people to protect themselves against bad weather, are linked to gods or spirits. The charms may be hung from ceilings, placed in fireplaces, or worn as jewellery.

Statue of Mayan rain god, Chac, used for worship

## STORMY TALE
In the Shinto religion that originated in Japan, Amaterasu Omikami is the "divine being who lights up heaven". Her brother is a storm god, and when he causes strong winds and floods, Amaterasu is so disappointed that she hides in a cave. This makes the world go dark, just as it seems to do during a storm.

*Bushy-tailed squirrel*

## FURRY TALE
Some people believe that the bushier a squirrel's tail during autumn, the harsher the winter will be. There is no scientific evidence that this idea is correct.

## WEATHER SACRIFICE
According to legend, the Mayan rain god, Chac, sent rain for the crops. But he also sent storms, which destroyed crops and flooded villages. People hoped that if they made offerings to Chac, the rains would continue to fall, but the storms would cease.

# Early forecasts

*Glass bulb*

THE MODERN SCIENCE of the weather is called meteorology. This science would not have been possible without discovering the behaviour of the elements – water, heat, and air – that make the weather. It was about 300 years ago that people first began to experiment scientifically with these elements. Through their experiments, they learnt about atmospheric pressure, which gases make up the air, and why water disappears as it evaporates. Early meteorologists invented a variety of crude measuring instruments that allowed them to test their theories, and devise new ones. Two of the most important developments were the thermometer for measuring temperatures, and the barometer, which measures atmospheric pressure. Another vital device is the hygrometer, which measures humidity – the concentration of water in the air. Nowadays, using sophisticated equipment, meteorologists can predict the arrival of extreme weather conditions, such as hurricanes, with great accuracy.

**UNDER PRESSURE**
In 1643, Italian physicist Evangelista Torricelli (1608–47) made the first barometer. He filled a 1-m (3-ft) long, glass tube with mercury, and placed it upside down in a bowl of mercury. The mercury dropped to about 80 cm (32 in). Torricelli realized that it was the weight, or pressure, of air on the mercury in the bowl that stopped the mercury in the tube from falling further.

**MOVING MERCURY**
The inventor of this mercury barometer was meteorologist Robert Fitzroy. His barometer has a scale in inches to measure the height of the mercury column. Fine weather is forecast when atmospheric pressure pushes the mercury column above 76 cm (30 in). Unsettled weather is likely when the mercury falls below this measurement.

Fitzroy barometer

**HIGH TEMPERATURE**
Italian physicist Galileo Galilei (1564–1642) designed this thermoscope, an early thermometer, about 400 years ago. It indicated changes in temperature but was unable to give exact readings. A long tube with a bulb at the end sat in a flask of water. Air in the bulb expanded as the temperature rose causing the water level in the tube to drop. The air contracted as it became cooler, raising the water level.

*Flask would have been filled with water*

*Cotton bag for absorbing moisture in the air*

**INVISIBLE WATER**
Air normally becomes very humid before a thunderstorm. The water in the air is an invisible vapour. You may not be able to see it, but you can measure it. This hygrometer, designed about 350 years ago, does just that. Water is absorbed from the air by the cotton bag, which becomes slightly heavier. The greater the humidity, the more the bag drops down.

*Balancing weight made of glass*

A 19th-century reproduction of Galileo's original thermoscope

17th-century balance hygrometer

*When the water level in the spout is high, air pressure is low, and storms can be expected*

*When working, the level of water in the weather glass would have been much higher*

*Scorch marks on card*

*Image of sun is reflected in the glass orb*

### PUSHING BOTH WAYS
This weather glass is a simple barometer. Atmospheric pressure pushes down on the water in the arm of the sealed flask. The air inside the flask pushes in the other direction. As atmospheric pressure changes, the level of water in the glass arm rises and falls. Before a storm, air pressure drops, and the water will rise further up the arm.

Sunshine recorder

### FOCUSED MEASUREMENT
This glass ball focuses sunlight to a point that scorches the paper behind it. As the sun moves across the sky during the day, the trail of scorches record how the amount of sunlight varies. When clouds pass in front of the sun, light is scattered in all directions, so there is not enough sunlight to scorch the paper.

### A QUESTION OF SCALE
When this thermometer was made, in 1657, there was no agreed scale for reading measurements. If you want to use a thermometer to take accurate temperatures, rather than just "hot" or "cold", your thermometer needs a scale. Today, meteorologists use two main scales to record temperature – Celsius and Fahrenheit. Both of these scales were invented in the 18th century.

*Thick needle aligns with the normal path of storms in the region*

*Thin needle indicates safe course away from the storm*

### KEEPING AN EYE ON THE STORM
Before radio warnings, sailors used this clever device, called a barocyclonometer, to calculate the position of approaching hurricanes. Cyclonic winds spiral at their centre, where the atmospheric pressure is very low. By measuring how atmospheric pressure and wind direction change, sailors could work out the general direction in which a hurricane was moving and steer their vessels to safety.

Ornate thermometer made in Italy, 1657

### HOTTING UP
The long, spiralling tube of this glass thermometer is designed to save space. When the temperature increases, water in the lower bulb expands, filling more space in the spiral tube. The higher the water level in the tube, the higher the temperature.

### IT'S A GAS
During the 1770s, French chemist Antoine Lavoisier (1743–94) made important discoveries about the atmosphere. He was the first person to discover that the atmosphere is a mixture of gases. He also found that hydrogen and oxgen combine to make water.

# What is extreme weather?

Hurricanes, tornadoes, droughts, floods, or freezing temperatures – extreme weather – can endanger people's lives or damage their crops or property. The weather at any time can be described by temperature, wind speed, atmospheric pressure, and precipitation (rain, hail, or snow). The average temperature of the world is about 21°C (70°F), but some places are much colder than this, other places much warmer. The average rainfall across the world is 100 cm (39 in) per year. But the rain is not evenly distributed – some parts of the world have virtually no rain at all, others as much as 11 m (36 ft) in one year. Also, a particular location may be dry for months and then be soaked by a flood. Often, extreme weather takes people by surprise. Destructive thunderstorms, tornadoes, or floods can happen in places where weather is normally quite calm.

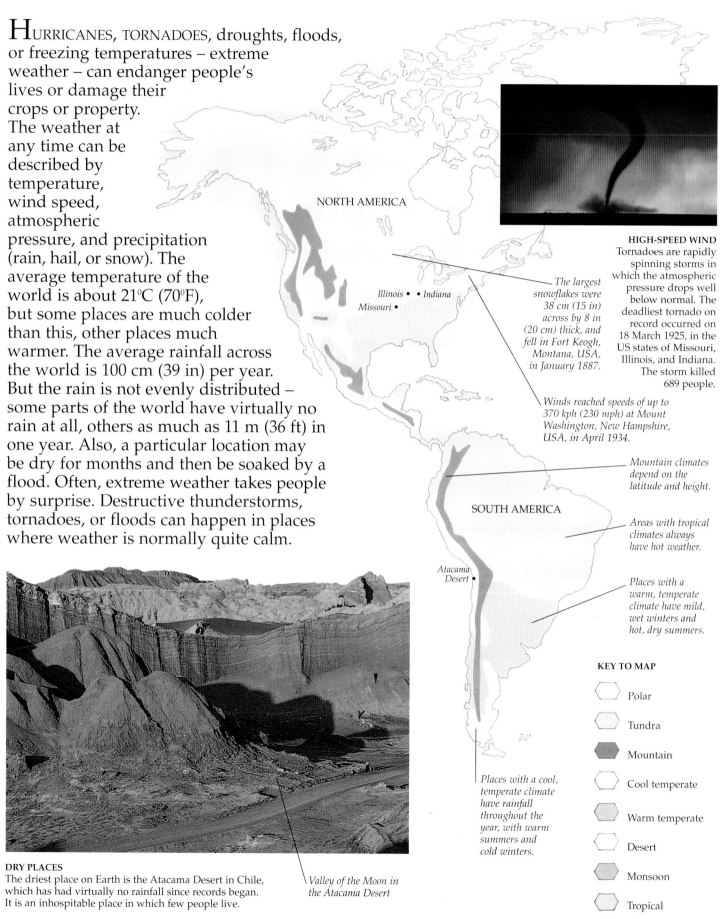

NORTH AMERICA

Illinois • • Indiana
Missouri •

*The largest snowflakes were 38 cm (15 in) across by 8 in (20 cm) thick, and fell in Fort Keogh, Montana, USA, in January 1887.*

**HIGH-SPEED WIND**
Tornadoes are rapidly spinning storms in which the atmospheric pressure drops well below normal. The deadliest tornado on record occurred on 18 March 1925, in the US states of Missouri, Illinois, and Indiana. The storm killed 689 people.

*Winds reached speeds of up to 370 kph (230 mph) at Mount Washington, New Hampshire, USA, in April 1934.*

*Mountain climates depend on the latitude and height.*

SOUTH AMERICA

*Areas with tropical climates always have hot weather.*

Atacama
Desert •

*Places with a warm, temperate climate have mild, wet winters and hot, dry summers.*

**KEY TO MAP**

⬡ Polar

⬡ Tundra

⬡ Mountain

⬡ Cool temperate

⬡ Warm temperate

⬡ Desert

⬡ Monsoon

⬡ Tropical

*Places with a cool, temperate climate have rainfall throughout the year, with warm summers and cold winters.*

**DRY PLACES**
The driest place on Earth is the Atacama Desert in Chile, which has had virtually no rainfall since records began. It is an inhospitable place in which few people live.

*Valley of the Moon in the Atacama Desert*

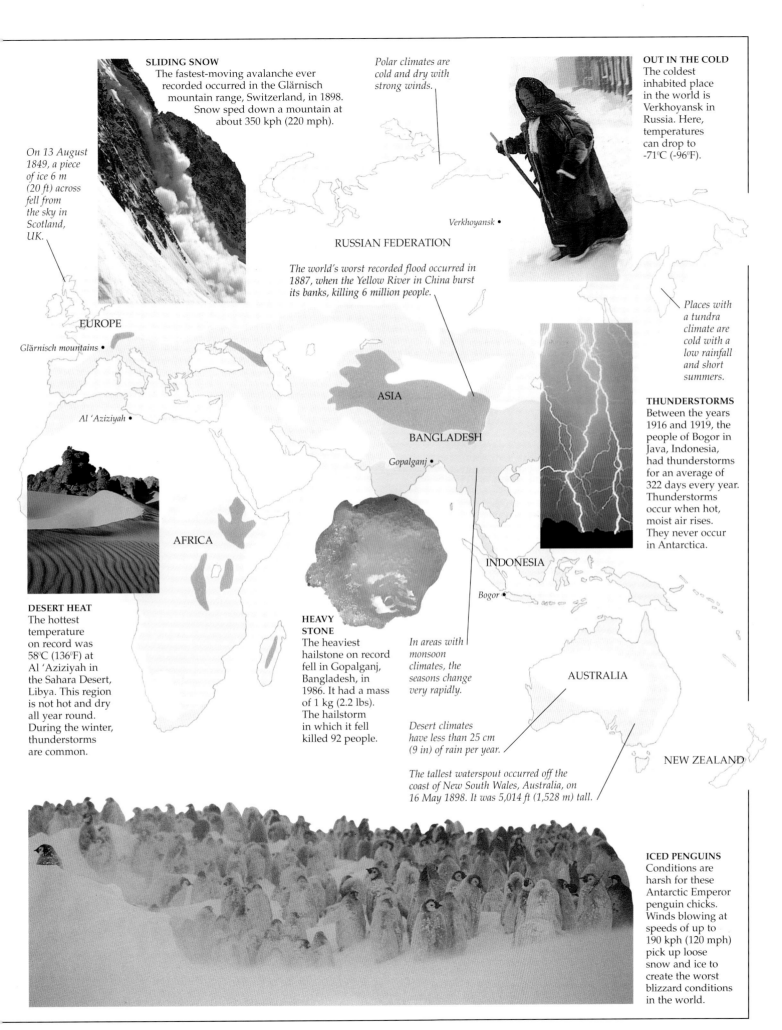

**SLIDING SNOW**
The fastest-moving avalanche ever recorded occurred in the Glärnisch mountain range, Switzerland, in 1898. Snow sped down a mountain at about 350 kph (220 mph).

*Polar climates are cold and dry with strong winds.*

**OUT IN THE COLD**
The coldest inhabited place in the world is Verkhoyansk in Russia. Here, temperatures can drop to -71°C (-96°F).

*On 13 August 1849, a piece of ice 6 m (20 ft) across fell from the sky in Scotland, UK.*

Verkhoyansk •

RUSSIAN FEDERATION

*The world's worst recorded flood occurred in 1887, when the Yellow River in China burst its banks, killing 6 million people.*

EUROPE

Glärnisch mountains •

*Places with a tundra climate are cold with a low rainfall and short summers.*

ASIA

Al 'Aziziyah •

BANGLADESH

Gopalganj •

**THUNDERSTORMS**
Between the years 1916 and 1919, the people of Bogor in Java, Indonesia, had thunderstorms for an average of 322 days every year. Thunderstorms occur when hot, moist air rises. They never occur in Antarctica.

AFRICA

INDONESIA

Bogor •

**DESERT HEAT**
The hottest temperature on record was 58°C (136°F) at Al 'Aziziyah in the Sahara Desert, Libya. This region is not hot and dry all year round. During the winter, thunderstorms are common.

**HEAVY STONE**
The heaviest hailstone on record fell in Gopalganj, Bangladesh, in 1986. It had a mass of 1 kg (2.2 lbs). The hailstorm in which it fell killed 92 people.

*In areas with monsoon climates, the seasons change very rapidly.*

AUSTRALIA

*Desert climates have less than 25 cm (9 in) of rain per year.*

NEW ZEALAND

*The tallest waterspout occurred off the coast of New South Wales, Australia, on 16 May 1898. It was 5,014 ft (1,528 m) tall.*

**ICED PENGUINS**
Conditions are harsh for these Antarctic Emperor penguin chicks. Winds blowing at speeds of up to 190 kph (120 mph) pick up loose snow and ice to create the worst blizzard conditions in the world.

# Causes of extreme weather

THERE ARE MANY FACTORS that can affect the weather. Among the most important are the heating of the Earth by the sun and differences in atmospheric pressure. Low atmospheric pressure usually means stormy weather. The pressure at the centre of a hurricane is extremely low, for example. Other factors, including dust from volcanoes or storms on the sun's surface, can disturb the weather, making it hotter or colder, or increasing or reducing rainfall. Humans can also affect the weather by polluting the atmosphere. Although the causes of extreme weather are well understood, it is still impossible to predict weather more than a few days ahead. This is because the weather is a very complex system, and even a small disturbance, such as the flutter of a butterfly's wing, can affect how the weather develops.

**CHAOTIC WEATHER**
While a butterfly cannot be said to cause floods and storms, it can, in theory, change the course of the weather. This is the strange conclusion of chaos theory – the study of unpredictable systems such as the weather. It is believed that the weather is so sensitive to atmospheric conditions that the slightest change in air movement, such as that caused by a tiny flapping wing, can alter the course of the world's weather.

**SPOTTING BAD WEATHER**
Dark, cool patches with a diameter of several thousand kilometres sometimes appear on the surface of the sun, and last for about a week. These sunspots throw out debris that can reach as far as Earth. When this happens, global temperatures can rise, and storms are more frequent. The spots are most numerous every 11 years, and extreme weather on Earth seems to coincide with this cycle.

**GLOBAL WARMING**
Many of the gases and smoke particles that modern industry and vehicles produce hang in the air. This can bring dramatic and beautiful sunsets, but can also affect the weather. Carbon dioxide released by burning fossil fuels seems to be causing an increase in the world's average temperature. If this "global warming"' continues, it could upset balances in the world's weather. There could be more storms, and the ice-caps may melt, raising sea levels.

**DEEP DEPRESSION**
This chart, called a barograph, shows a depression over the British Isles. One of the common features of unsettled weather is a region of air with low atmospheric pressure. This is called a depression, because a lowering of air pressure reduces, or "depresses", the reading on a barometer. A depression forms when air is warmed, expands, and rises. Winds spiral in towards the centre of the depression. The deeper the depression, the stronger the winds.

**GREENHOUSE GASES**
Chemical compounds called chlorofluorocarbons (CFCs) are released by various industrial processes, and used to be emitted by aerosol cans. CFCs break down an atmospheric gas called ozone, which protects the Earth from harmful ultraviolet radiation. Like carbon dioxide, CFCs are known as "greenhouse gases" because they seem to slowly increase the world's temperature. During the 1990s, most of the world's nations agreed to stop producing CFCs, and aerosol sprays were banned.

**HOT AND COLD**
The sun is the source of most of the Earth's energy, but some parts of the world receive more energy than others. At the poles, sunlight always hits the Earth's surface at an angle, because of the curvature of the globe. The sun therefore heats the equator more intensely than it does the poles. These temperature differences alter atmospheric pressure. This causes global winds that influence weather patterns.

Equator

*Sunlight warms the Earth*

*Sunlight is concentrated at the equator*

*Sunlight spreads over a greater area at the north and south poles*

**GLOBAL COOLING**
Mount St Helens (right) in Washington, USA, erupted in 1980. For a few months after the event, climatologists measured a drop of almost 0.5°C (33°F) in the average global temperature. This was due to volcanic dust travelling around the world and blocking out some of the sun's heat and light.

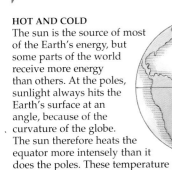

# Severe winds

STRONG WINDS CAN WREAK HAVOC. Their force depends on the speed at which they travel. The fastest winds at ground or sea level are found in hurricanes and tornadoes, and both can cause widespread devastation. Higher in the atmosphere are winds that are faster still – jet streams. They are too high up to cause any damage, and are very important because they help to distribute the sun's heat around the world. Global winds are caused by the sun heating various parts of the Earth differently. Local winds, on the other hand, are smaller-scale, and are caused by regional changes in temperature and pressure. To predict wind behaviour, accurate speed measurements are vital.

**ALL AT SEA**
Francis Beaufort (1774–1857) was a commander in the British Navy. In 1805 he devised a system – the Beaufort Scale – for estimating wind speeds at sea. The system assigns names and numbers to 12 different strengths of wind, from "light air" to "hurricane force". It is still in use today, but modern devices are more accurate.

**STANDING TALL**
This model shows the design for the 840-m (2,700-ft) tall Millennium Tower planned for Tokyo, Japan. One of the most important considerations in the design of any skyscraper is wind resistance. Millennium Tower is encircled by a steel frame, which strengthens the building and provides protection from fierce winds.

Architectural model of
Millennium Tower, Tokyo

*Head faces in the direction from which the wind is blowing*

**WEATHER VANE**
Weather vanes are perhaps the oldest of all meteorological instruments. This weather cock's tail has a larger surface area than its head. The tail swings around as the wind changes direction, and points the cock's head towards the wind. A reading is taken from the direction in which the wind blows. For example, a westerly wind is one that comes from the west and blows to the east.

**FLYING IN THE WIND**
In March 1999, balloonists Bertrand Piccard and Brian Jones became the first people ever to fly a hot-air balloon nonstop around the world. Their balloon, *Breitling Orbiter 3*, was sometimes assisted by jet-stream winds blowing at up to 300 kph (185 mph). Jet streams can reduce aeroplane flight times from the United States to Europe by up to two hours.

**WIND SWEPT**
A combination of wind and sand erosion has carved a beautiful landscape into these sandstone rocks. If severe winds blow across the rocks, sweeping up the surface layer of sand, dense and dangerous sandstorms may occur.

**Wind vane to show direction**

**Cups spin around – their speed depends on the strength of the wind**

**Rotors turn wind vane into the wind**

**Average wind speed is recorded on graph paper as the cylinder rotates**

**A man struggles across Chicago's Wabash Avenue Bridge in fierce winds**

### WIND RECORDER
This clever measuring device was made long before electronic computers existed. It is called an anemometer and records wind speed and direction over a long period of time. In order to understand how the wind works, forecasters need to take as many measurements as possible.

Weathered sandstone, Colorado Plateau, Utah, USA

### THE WINDY CITY
During winter, the US city of Chicago is regularly battered by strong winds. Chicago lies near the Great Lakes, where inland air mixes with air from the lakes. Because the atmospheric pressure of these air masses is different, they send gusts of wind around the city as they collide.

### SWING BRIDGE
Tacoma Narrows Bridge in Washington, USA, was badly damaged by wind in 1940. Strong gusts caused the bridge to swing – first gently, and then ever more violently. Eventually, the bridge collapsed. Since the winds were not as strong as in a hurricane, the bridge's design was blamed for the disaster.

# Thunderous storms

TREMENDOUS AMOUNTS OF ENERGY are released in the torrential rain, strong winds, thunder, and lightning that accompany thunderstorms. The most energetic storms may create hail or even tornadoes. The source of all this energy is the sun, which evaporates water from land or sea. The resulting warm, moist air rises and begins to cool as it does so. Vapour in the cooling air condenses, forming countless tiny water drops and ice crystals that make up a darkening cumulonimbus cloud, or thunderhead. The rising current of air is known as an updraught, and may reach speeds of more than 100 kph (60 mph). When rain or hail falls, it brings with it a downdraught of cooler air. The downdraught spreads out in all directions when it reaches the ground, causing the gusty winds of a thunderstorm.

**LETTING GO**
Tornadoes, lightning, and inland waterspouts often occur during severe storms as thunderclouds quickly release energy. The large lightning bolt and waterspout seen here occurred during a thunderstorm over Florida, USA.

**VIEW FROM THE AIR**
This photograph was taken from a spacecraft orbiting around Earth. It shows how a whole system of storms can develop when warm, moist air meets cold, dry air. The cold air undercuts the warm air, lifting it to form pockets of rising air. These pockets show up as thunderheads through the existing blanket of cloud.

**WATER CARRIER**
A thunderhead is an impressive tower of cloud. The top of the cloud may reach a height of some 12 km (7.5 miles), while its base may loom just 1,000 m (3,280 ft) above ground. A typical thunderhead contains about 10,000 tonnes of water.

## THUNDER BEATS

Balls of
thunder

Thunder
shown as
a demon
in the air

Drumstick
to beat out
the sound
of thunder

In the Japanese
Shinto religion, many
forces of nature are
worshipped as
gods, known as *kami*.
Sometimes *kami* are
represented as human
figures. This Japanese
god of thunder is
shown as a strong
man beating
his drum.

Japanese
thunder god

- Ice particles
- Snowflakes
- Water drops

Hot, moist
air rises

Heavy rain and
maybe hail

Cloud begins to
run out of energy

## LIFE OF A THUNDERSTORM

This diagram explains how a
thunderstorm develops. First,
an updraught (red arrows) of
warm, moist air begins to form
the cloud as the moisture
evaporates from the air. Water
vapour then releases large
amounts of heat as it
condenses. This heat warms
the air further and causes the
air to rise higher. The storm
finally subsides when the
air begins to cool and the
downdraught (green arrows)
helps to disperse the cloud.

## CALM BEFORE THE STORM

Thunderstorms often occur at the end of a hot summer day, when air that has been warmed
by the hot ground rises quickly into the cooling air. A thundercloud carries many tonnes of
water. These clouds are so dense that they absorb almost all of the light that falls on them.
This is why they appear black. Beyond the thunderclouds, the air is clear and calm.

Supercell storm cloud
in Texas, USA

Cloud stops rising and
spreads out as it hits a cold
dry layer of atmospheric air

## SUPERCELL

Most thunderstorms
begin as one or more
cells (pockets) of
rising air. The
term "supercell"
is used to describe
a particularly large
and energetic cell, in
which air rises more
quickly than normal. This
type of cell carries a huge
amount of water up into
the thundercloud. Tornadoes
and waterspouts are born
from such cells.

Strong updraughts
carry wisps of cloud
high into the atmosphere

Mixture
of ice
crystals
and water

Air is drawn in at
the base of the cloud

# Twisting tornadoes

TORNADOES HAVE MANY NAMES including whirlwinds and twisters. These high-speed spiralling winds roar past in just a few minutes, but leave behind them a trail of destruction. A tornado is born at the base of a thundercloud, as warm, moist air rises from the ground and passes through a mass of colder air at the bottom of the cloud. This updraught rubs against the heavier cold air, and the Earth's rotation causes the air to revolve – just as water spins as it runs down the plug hole. The pressure at the centre of a tornado is much lower than that outside. This creates a funnel, or vortex, which acts like a giant vacuum cleaner, sucking up anything in its path. These deadly tornadoes may strike wherever thunderstorms occur.

*A tornado funnel appears at the base of a thundercloud*

**1 WALL OF CLOUD**
This series of photographs clearly shows how a tornado develops. The funnel of the tornado descends from a thundercloud above. A column of cloud then forms as moisture as the air condenses in the low pressure inside the tornado.

*Swirling black thundercloud indicates the start of a tornado*

*Funnel changes colour as it picks up debris*

**2 DOWN TO EARTH**
This tornado is passing over dusty farmland. So, when the base of the tornado meets the ground, the funnel becomes partly obscured by dust picked up by the rising air and swirling winds.

**LIQUID FUNNEL**
When a tornado passes over a lake or the sea, the updraught at its centre sucks up water, forming a waterspout. The wind speeds inside a waterspout are much less than in ordinary tornadoes – as low as 80 kph (50 mph) – partly due to the weight of the water they carry.

*Funnel narrows as the tornado's energy diminishes*

**3 LOSING POWER**
Energy from the tornado's winds throws debris into the air. As the tornado loses energy, it slows down. Eventually, the funnel will shrink back to the thundercloud from which it was born.

**STRANGE DOWNPOURS**
When a tornado passes over water, small animals such as frogs and fish may be lifted high into the air, only to fall to Earth again some distance away once the tornado loses its energy.

## SPIN CYCLE

A tornado is a writhing funnel of rapidly spinning air that descends to the ground from the base of a large thundercloud. At the heart of a tornado is a low-pressure vortex, which acts like a huge vacuum cleaner, sucking up air and anything the tornado encounters on the ground.

## KICKING UP DUST

Dust devils, like waterspouts, are whirlwinds, which are common in desert regions. Although less energetic and less destructive than tornadoes, they are created in the same way. Air above the hot desert sand begins to rise quickly, producing the updraught necessary for the whirlwind to form. The circling winds typically reach speeds of about 40 kph (25 mph).

# Tornado force

THE
VIOLENT
SWIRLING
WINDS of a
tornado are
among the most
destructive forces in
nature. With speeds of up
to 500 kph (310 mph), these
winds can tear houses apart,
wrap cars around trees, and kill or
injure any living thing in their path.
A violent tornado can devastate a whole
community, destroying all the buildings
in its path. Most of the world's destructive
tornadoes occur during the summer in the
mid-western states of the USA, where cold air
from Canada in the north sits on top of warm,
moist air from the Gulf of Mexico to the south.
This region is often referred to as Tornado Alley.
Meteorologists still cannot fully explain the
mechanisms that cause tornadoes, and
predicting where and when they will
occur proves even more difficult.

## TOWERING TORNADO
The destructive vortex
(spinning centre) of a
tornado is usually about
2 km (1 mile) wide. Dust
or objects at ground level
are lifted high into the air
and are flung sideways or
kept in the air to be deposited
later when the tornado winds
down. Tornadoes typically sweep
over the land at speeds of about
55 kph (35 mph), leaving behind
them a trail of devastation.

*Venetian
blind twisted
by a tornado*

*Tornado funnel descends
from a thundercloud*

## BLIND PANIC
The air pressure inside a tornado
is much lower than normal. When
a tornado passed by this window,
the window exploded outwards,
because air pressure inside the
room was higher than outside.
Much of the destruction of a
tornado is caused by the sudden
drop in pressure that it brings.

*This door was sucked out of the
window by the tornado's force*

## TORNADO ALLEY
This map
highlights an area
in the United States
known as Tornado
Alley, which includes
parts of the states of
Kansas, Oklahoma,
and Missouri. This
region experiences several
hundred tornadoes every
year. Tornadoes claim about
100 lives each year in the
United States.

CANADA

UNITED
STATES

*Kansas* • *Missouri*
• *Oklahoma*

MEXICO

Areas most
at risk from
tornadoes

**BLOWN AWAY**
The worshippers in this church in Piedmont, Virginia, USA, were caught by surprise when a tornado struck during a service, in March 1994. The force of the tornado ripped the roof off the church.

*Dust and debris
is swept up as
the tornado passes
over the ground*

**IN A TWIST**
The incredible power of a tornado is shown in this photograph of what was once a truck. Winds travelling at more than 400 kph (250 mph) picked up the truck and hurled it down again, leaving behind a mess of twisted steel.

*Twisting
column of
cloud*

*Swirling vortex*

*A tornado rips
a house apart
in the 1998
film Twister*

**STORM CHASING**
In the United States some people deliberately pursue tornadoes in order to learn more about them. These storm chasers, in their specially equipped trucks, are called into action when a "tornado watch" warning is issued by the National Weather Service.

**CIRCLES OF MYSTERY**
For centuries, strange and unexplained circles of flattened crops have appeared in fields across the world. Some people believe that tornadoes are responsible for many of these circles. But this is unlikely since tornadoes do not tend to hover over one spot for long enough – instead, they move across the land, leaving a trail of destruction.

**STRANGE TALES**
Tornadoes often leave behind bizarre stories. A chicken in Alabama, USA, is reported to have survived tornadic winds of about 200 kph (120 mph), which stripped it of its tail and feathers.

# Lightning strikes

NEARLY TWO THOUSAND thunderstorms occur at any one time across the world. The most impressive feature of a thunderstorm is lightning. Flashes and bolts of lightning are caused by an electric charge that builds up inside a thundercloud. Air inside the cloud rises at speeds of up to 100 kph (60 mph). Tiny ice crystals are carried to the top of the cloud by the moving air, rubbing against pellets of hail as they do so. The ice crystals become positively charged while the hail becomes negatively charged. A lightning bolt is the way in which the electric charges are neutralized – simply huge sparks between cloud and ground, or between the top and bottom of a cloud. The most common form of lightning is fork lightning, but there are other, less common forms, such as ribbon lightning.

**STORMY GOD**
Before scientists began to explain weather patterns, many cultures believed that the weather was controlled by gods. The Norse god of thunder, Thor, was believed to have made thunderbolts with his magic hammer.

Fossilized lightning bolt

**SAND SCULPTURE**
This strange shape is made of sand that has melted and then solidified in the path of a lightning strike. The resulting mineral is called fulgurite. The temperature inside a bolt of lightning reaches 30,000°C (54,000°F) – about five times the temperature of the surface of the sun.

**BRIGHT SPARK**
During a thunderstorm, in 1752, American politician and scientist Benjamin Franklin carried out a dangerous experiment. He flew a kite, with metal objects attached to its string, high into the sky. The metal items produced sparks, proving that electricity had passed along the wet string.

**PERSONAL SAFETY**
An interesting fashion accessory of the 18th century was the Franklin wire. Invented by Benjamin Franklin in 1753, the metallic wire was suspended from an umbrella or hat and dragged along the ground to divert lightning strikes away from the wearer.

*Lightning conductors were all the rage in Paris, 1778*

**LIGHTNING RODS**
Tall buildings, such as the Eiffel Tower (above) in Paris, France, are regular targets for lightning strikes. Metal rods called lightning conductors protect buildings to which they are attached by conducting the electricity safely to the ground.

*This tree has been torn apart by lightning*

## QUICK AS A FLASH

Time-lapse photography captured the many successive lightning flashes of this storm in the USA. A lightning strike begins as an invisible "leader stroke" at the base of a thundercloud. The leader stroke forms a path of charged atoms, along which huge quantities of electric charge pass incredibly quickly, producing a bright glow. The temperature of the air along this path heats up rapidly and expands, creating a shock wave that is heard as a loud thunderclap.

## FORCE OF LIGHTNING

The power of lightning can virtually demolish a building or kill outright a person or animal unfortunate enough to be struck. Trees are particularly vulnerable to lightning strikes because the moist layer below the bark acts as a conductor.

*Cloud illuminated from within by a lightning bolt*

## SKY LIGHTS

Most bolts of lightning do not strike at ground level – they occur within a cloud. A powerful electric current passes between the positively charged top of the cloud, and its negatively charged base. Sometimes, lightning can pass between two neighbouring clouds.

# Hailstorms

BALLS OF ICE CALLED HAILSTONES are produced during thunderstorms. The strong vertical air currents in a thundercloud force lumps of ice up and down inside the cloud. With each upward movement the hailstones collect another layer of ice. They continue to grow in size until they are too big to be lifted again by the up-currents. The stronger the up-current, the heavier a hailstone can become. Individual stones with a mass of more than 700 g (1.6 lbs) have been recorded. Stones of this weight require an updraught of more than 150 kph (95 mph). Hailstones that heavy can be life-threatening, but any hailstorm can cause serious damage. Among the worst storms in recent history was one that occurred in Munich, Germany, in July 1984. Financial losses were estimated to have totalled £625 million ($1 billion).

Combating hail in cotton fields in the Fergana Valley, Russia

**CLOUD BURSTING**
People in many parts of the world have searched for ways to save their crops from hail damage. The Russians have, perhaps, had the most success. By firing chemical substances into thunderclouds they have been able to make potential hail fall as harmless rain. This technique has saved vast prairies of grain that could otherwise have been flattened by hail within minutes.

**HEAVY STORM**
Hailstones are usually about the size of a pea. They bounce when they hit a hard surface, and tend to settle, forming a strange ice-white carpet. Stones do, however, vary in size, and storms vary in severity. In the USA alone, a single hailstorm can cause property damage in excess of £300 million ($500 million), and crop damage amounting to about £185 million ($300 million).

*Maize crop destroyed by a severe hailstorm*

**HAIL ALLEY**
Vast regions of the US are under the constant threat of hailstorms. One area in particular, a belt of land spanning from Texas to Montana, known as "Hail Alley", regularly experiences severe hailstorms. Farmers in this region need to spend huge amounts on hail insurance. Yet, little has been done in the US to explore methods of crop protection.

*Vehicles pelted by hail during a storm in Texas, USA, in May 1977*

**DANGEROUS DRIVING**
Driving through a hailstorm is extremely hazardous because vehicles skid easily on the hard, icy stones. The severity of damage caused by falling hail depends on the wind speed during a storm. Hailstones with a diameter of 10 cm (4 in), such as the one that hit this windscreen, travel at speeds of up to 170 kph (106 mph).

**ICE PACK**
Hailstones are made up of layers – a bit like onions. Each layer represents one journey through the cloud in which the stone formed. This hailstone – one of the largest ever found – had a diameter of about 19 cm (7.5 in), and a mass of 766 g (1.67 lbs). It has been cut in half and photographed through polarizing filters to show the layers inside the stone.

*Windscreen shattered by a hailstone during a storm near Burlington, Colorado, USA, in 1990*

*This hailstone is the size of a grapefruit*

**BIG CHILL**
Large hailstones normally fall from "supercell" thunderclouds, which typically have one very strong updraught. This 10-cm (4-in) diameter hailstone fell near Breckenridge in Colorado, USA, in May 1978.

*Cross-section of a hailstone*

*Drivers park their vehicles at the side of the road as they wait for the danger to pass*

# Hurricane alert

THE WORD "HURRICANE" has many origins, including the Native American Taino word "hurucane", meaning "evil spirit of the wind". Hurricanes are officially called "tropical cyclones", but also have several other names, including cyclones in the Indian Ocean, and typhoons in the Pacific. They are huge, rotating storms, which can bring widespread devastation, with winds of up to 350 kph (210 mph), heavy rain, and stormy seas. A hurricane begins as a region of heated air over the warm seas in the tropics – parts of the world near the equator. The heated air expands and rises, creating an area of low pressure air. The surrounding air moves in towards the lower pressure, and is made to spin by the Earth's rotation. Predicting hurricanes is not easy, but weather satellites enable forecasters to give a few days' advance warning.

**WINDY WARNING**
The destruction caused by a hurricane can be reduced, and lives saved, if a warning is given. These flags are one way to alert people to hurricane danger.

*Many buildings were wrecked when a cyclone hit Albany, Georgia, USA (1940)*

**GALE FORCE**
The destructive force of a hurricane comes largely from its strong winds, which spiral in towards the centre of the storm. As more and more air is drawn in towards the centre of the storm, wind speeds increase – just as ice-skaters can spin faster by tucking in their arms.

*19th-century aneroid barometer*

**UNDER PRESSURE**
A barometer shows the push of the air, caused by the weight of the atmosphere – this push is called atmospheric pressure. The pressure is very low in a hurricane, and changes in pressure can help forecasters to predict approaching storms.

**WHEELED WARNING**
In areas where few people have radios or televisions, warnings may be delivered in other ways. This man is cycling around a village in Bangladesh, using a megaphone to shout out a hurricane warning.

**WATER, WATER EVERYWHERE**
Under the low pressure air at the centre of the storm, the sea level bulges to as much as 3 m (12 ft) higher than normal. This swell of water can submerge large areas of coastline, and is responsible for most of the deaths caused by hurricanes.

*A community in Bangladesh waits for the threat of a hurricane to pass*

*Stilts raise this purpose-built cyclone shelter above the ground*

**SAFETY ON STILTS**
Floods are very common during a hurricane – from heavy rains and, in coastal areas, high waves from stormy seas. This shelter is raised above the ground so that flood waters can pass beneath it without endangering lives. The building is specially designed to withstand high winds.

Northern hemisphere

Equator

NEW GUINEA

AUSTRALIA

Southern hemisphere

**SPINNING CYCLONES**

Hurricanes can form at any time in the warm tropics, and are a type of tropical cyclone. A cyclone is an area of low pressure air with winds that spiral inwards – clockwise in the southern hemisphere and anti-clockwise in the northern hemisphere. Hurricanes move westwards away from the equator. They never occur on the equator itself.

**VIEW FROM ABOVE**

Hurricanes form where the temperature of the sea is above 27°C (80°F). A low pressure, or depression, forms and, once wind speeds reach 62 kph (39 mph), it is classified as a tropical storm. When winds reach 118 kph (74 mph), the storm becomes a hurricane. A hurricane picks up about two billion tonnes of water, as vapour, from the ocean each day. This vapour condenses to form clouds, such as those shown right. One bizarre feature of a hurricane is its eye, or centre. Conditions in the eye are very calm, while all around it are thick clouds and high-speed winds.

*The eye of a storm can be up to 50 km (32 miles) wide*

Satellite view of Hurricane Emilia (1994)

# Hurricane horror

SOME REGIONS OF THE WORLD are more prone to hurricane devastation than others. Areas outside the tropics – more than 2,500 km (1,500 miles) from the equator – are much less at risk than tropical regions. This is because the seas are cooler far from the equator, providing less energy to fuel hurricanes. The northeast coast of South America is an area often hit because it lies in the path of hurricanes that form just north of the equator, and move northwest in the Atlantic Ocean. Hurricanes bring huge waves, known as storm surges, which cause the biggest loss of lives. But it is the strong winds that cause the greatest destruction – they have no regard for people's homes or possessions.

*The hurricane of 1900 demolished this school in Galveston, but the desks are still screwed tightly to the floor*

**AMERICAN TRAGEDY**
One of the deadliest hurricanes experienced in the US struck the coastal city of Galveston, Texas, in September 1900. More than 12,000 people died, 2,600 homes were destroyed, and about 10,000 people were left homeless. A protective wall was constructed around the rebuilt city, and has successfully protected it from hurricane tidal waves ever since.

*Hurricane David's powerful winds have lifted this plane into the air, and deposited it on top of a hangar*

**ROOFTOP LANDING**
The Dominican Republic was struck by a particularly dangerous and destructive hurricane in August 1979. Named Hurricane David, the storm reached speeds of up to 277 kph (172 mph), and lasted for two weeks. During that time, the island's coastlines were bombarded by huge waves, and 1,300 people lost their lives.

*A low, flat, and well-secured roof helped this house to survive almost entirely intact*

## IN THE BUNKER

Flood waters produced by Hurricane Hugo in 1989 swept this boat from its harbour mooring to a nearby golf course. Hugo hit the Virgin Islands first. It then moved over warm water, where it gained more energy, and then struck South Carolina, in the USA.

## REDUCED TO RUBBLE

In April 1991, a hurricane called Cyclone 2B crept up the Bay of Bengal and wreaked havoc on the people of Bangladesh. The storm brought with it 240-kph (150-mph) winds and a ferocious 6-m (20-ft) tidal wave. The winds reduced thousands of homes to rubble, while floods claimed the lives of over 140,000 people.

## WAVE POWER

Vast areas of the US were flooded when Hurricane Floyd struck in 1999. At the centre of every hurricane is a swell, or bulge, of water up to 3 m (10 ft) high. This is because the atmospheric pressure at the heart of a hurricane is very low. If a hurricane moves close to land, the swell becomes a wave that can cause flooding, crop damage, and loss of life.

## WITHOUT WARNING

In late December 1974, Cyclone Tracy formed 500 km (310 miles) northeast of the Australian coast. The local Tropical Cyclone Warning Centre tracked the storm – it seemed that the hurricane would miss land. Unexpectedly, in the early hours of Christmas Day, it turned and approached the town of Darwin. About 90 per cent of the town's buildings were destroyed, leaving half of its 40,000 residents homeless. Within a week of the disaster, over 20,000 people had been airlifted to other parts of the country.

## I WILL SURVIVE

In August 1992, Hurricane Andrew caused extensive damage throughout the Bahamas, Louisiana, and Florida in the USA. The hurricane caused 52 deaths and about $22 billion in damage. It ravaged many towns, and left thousands of people homeless. The lucky resident of this house in Florida, however, was proud to have lived through the fierce storms.

# Fog and smog

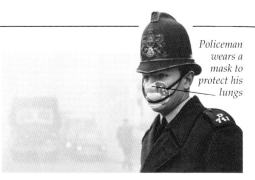

WHEN THE AIR IS FULL of moisture and the temperature drops, fog may occur. Fog is simply cloud at ground level. It consists of countless tiny droplets of water suspended in the air. Light passing through fog scatters in every direction, making it translucent, like tracing paper. In thick fog, visibility can be reduced to less than a few metres. Travel in these conditions is treacherous and accidents on the roads, at sea, or in the air are common. Not much can be done to reduce the danger, but foghorns or radar can locate ships and aeroplanes, and lighthouses and traffic signals can help to guide them to safety. Fog costs airlines millions of pounds each year through airport shutdowns. When fog combines with smoke, a thick and dangerous mixture, called smog, may form.

**PEA-SOUPER**
Until the 1960s, London, England, suffered frequent and serious smog caused by the burning of coal. These smogs, nicknamed "pea-soupers", caused serious, and often fatal, respiratory (breathing) problems. The city was cured of this problem by The Clean Air Acts of 1956 and 1968, which forced people to use "smokeless fuel".

**CLEAR FOR TAKE-OFF**
During World War II, a method was devised to clear fog from airport runways. Huge amounts of kerosene were burned to provide heat. The heat turned the water droplets in the fog into invisible vapour. This method was successful, but is seldom used today, because it is very expensive and can be dangerous.

*Member of airport staff ignites fog burners*

**WATER CATCHERS**
For residents of Chungungo village, Chile, frequent fog is actually a blessing. These long plastic fences just outside the village catch water from fog that blows in from the sea. Chungungo lies in a very dry location, and the water that the fences collect provides much of the village's water supply.

*Sulphurous fog hangs over Christchurch in New Zealand*

**CLEANING UP THE AIR**
Sulphurous smog hangs in the air above many towns and cities. This type of smog is produced when smoke from burning fuels combines with fog. On calm days, smog may linger for many hours, endangering health and proving treacherous to traffic. Nowadays, sulphurous smogs are less common due to city dwellers burning cleaner fuels. But equally deadly is "photochemical smog" caused by sunlight combining with air-pollutants.

*Gas container*

*Loud noise travels through this horn*

**SOUNDING
THE ALARM**
Thick sea-fog can be hazardous to sailors. Gas released through the nozzle of this foghorn makes a very loud noise that can be heard clearly through the fog. This gives other sailors a chance to avoid a possible collision with a vessel that they cannot yet see. Large ships have huge, deafening foghorns that can be heard over many kilometres.

*Golden Gate Bridge in San Francisco, USA, is hidden beneath a blanket of fog*

**FOGTOWN**
San Francisco in the USA is sometimes referred to as "Fog City". The city is famous for its summer fog, which occurs when warm, moist air meets the cool water that travels into San Francisco Bay from further down the coast. This chilly fog normally lingers until about midday.

**LIGHTING THE WAY**
Before the invention of radar, sailors had no way of seeing ahead of them in thick sea-fogs. Lighthouses, like this one at the George Washington Bridge in New York, USA, gave sailors plenty of warning of the dangers ahead. By flashing a powerful beam of light during fogs and at night, lighthouses guided ships away from rocks or shallow water.

# High seas

THE SEA COVERS about two-thirds of our planet. Strong winds constantly disturb the surface of the oceans, producing waves that break as they reach the shore. During severe storms, particularly hurricanes, sea water can cause widespread flooding. Many scientists fear that global warming will cause more of the ice-caps to melt resulting in an overall rise in sea levels. This threatens to increase the risk of serious flooding during storms at high tide in many coastal locations. But it is not only on the coast that people are at risk. Ships can sink in stormy weather, leaving passengers stranded in dangerous waters. Neither is it only people and their properties that are at risk from the sea – waves are continuously eroding the coastline.

**IN DEEP WATER**
High seas are normally stormy seas, with dangerous waves that can sink a ship or leave it stranded. Air-sea rescue helicopters rush to the aid of survivors. The helicopters hover above the sea while a rescuer is lowered on a winch to lift the survivors clear of the water.

*A rescuer is lowered to the sea by a search and rescue helicopter*

*Collapsed coastal road caused by wave erosion*

**TEARING ALONG**
Crashing waves wreak havoc on coastlines. They dissolve pieces of rock and break off parts of cliffs. The stormier the sea, and the higher its level, the greater the erosion. If global warming continues, sea levels will rise, increasing the rate of erosion and the risk of flooding.

**HOLDING BACK**
The Thames River Barrier in London, UK, aims to protect the city from flooding until at least 2050. As sea levels rise, the threat of flooding in southern England is increasing. Ten huge gates can be raised when sea levels surge. These gates prevent water from travelling up the river towards London.

**UNWELCOME VISITOR**
This devastation on Okushiri Island, Japan, was caused by a huge, powerful wave called a tsunami. Tsunamis, often mistakenly called tidal waves, are triggered by vibrations from earthquakes beneath the seabed.

**STORMY SEA**
When Hurricane Hugo hit the West Indies and southeastern USA in 1989, it produced a surge 2 m (6 ft) high in open water. This rose to 6 m (18 ft) in some places, where the water was funnelled up along valleys. The sudden and dramatic surge in sea level when a hurricane reaches land is caused by low air pressure at the storm's centre.

**WALL OF WATER**

An ocean wave begins as wind blows across the sea's surface, making the water swing up and down, and back and forth. When the wave nears the shore, where the sea becomes shallower, the movement is "broken", and the water topples over, forming a breaker. Huge breakers, such as this one, are sometimes called dumpers. They send water crashing in all directions if they hit the shore.

*This huge plunging wave is on the verge of breaking*

# Snowstorms

EXTREMELY COLD CONDITIONS can endanger the lives of people and animals. A heavy snowfall can make roads impassable or bury buildings, particularly when the wind blows the snow into piles, called snowdrifts. Snow and strong winds cause blizzards, which reduce visibility, and make travel by road treacherous. When the temperature falls below freezing point – 0°C (32°F) – snow will settle on the ground. Snowflakes are clumps of tiny ice crystals produced inside a cloud. These crystals form as water vapour freezes around tiny specks of mineral dust in the atmosphere. Ice storms occur when water in the air freezes to form icy fog at ground level. Everything becomes coated in an icy layer. The ice can become so thick that trees collapse under the weight.

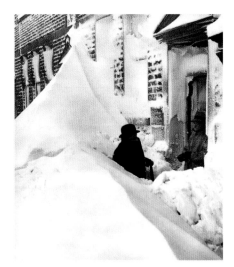

**PILED HIGH**
Snow has piled up against the side of this house in Derbyshire, England, obscuring ground-floor windows and making it difficult to reach the front door. Snowdrifts, such as this, form when snow carried by the wind is stopped in its tracks by an obstacle.

Ice crystal from a snowflake

**WHAT IS SNOW?**
The ice crystals that make up snowflakes are too small to see with the naked eye. Their beautiful symmetrical shapes can, however, be viewed through a microscope. No two snowflakes are the same because their growth within a cloud depends on temperature, humidity, and air currents. These conditions are never identical for any two snowflakes.

**WHITE-OUT**
Blizzard conditions have forced these drivers to stop their cars. If they remain in their vehicles, they can be found more easily, but they may find warmth and shelter if there are houses or other buildings nearby. One person froze to death during this particular snowstorm, near Caen in France.

*Blade of a snowplough clearing a road in France*

**CLEARING THE WAY**
In areas where heavy snow is common, snowploughs keep major roads clear. Drivers use tyre chains for a better grip. But for unprepared communities, a sudden snowfall can cause chaos. Tyres easily lose their grip and accidents are common.

## FROZEN DRIPS
Icicles are a common sight on very cold days. They form as water drips from ridges, such as rooftops or the branches of trees. The drips do not freeze all at once. Instead, only a small amount freezes, while the rest drips off. Part of the next drip freezes, too, and gradually an icicle builds up.

## WIND CHILL
This man's face-warmer froze as he shovelled snow outside his home in Milwaukee, Wisconsin, USA. The temperature during this severe winter storm, in December 1995, was -35°C (-30°F), but the "wind chill" made it feel like -70°C (-90°F). Wind chill occurs on a windy day, when heat passes from your warm body to cold air more quickly than on a calm day, making the temperature feel even lower than it is in reality. Wearing several layers of clothing, covering as much of your body as possible, is the best way to keep warm, and prevent frostbite.

*Icicles hang from a cliff during an ice storm in Arizona, USA*

## STAYING INDOORS
Extreme cold weather can close down schools and businesses, and force people to stay indoors for safety and warmth. Vehicles may become frozen solid and aeroplanes may be unable to take off due to ice on the wings. This car was covered in a sheet of ice during a severe winter storm in northeast Canada, when the temperature dropped to -29°C (-20°F). During the storm, trees fell down under the weight of ice, and tens of thousands of cattle froze to death.

**WATCHING FOR SIGNS**

Most mountain resorts have some way of alerting people to avalanche danger. Although difficult to predict exactly where and when an avalanche will strike, by examining the snow, experts can tell when an area is at risk.

*This crack marks the start of a slab avalanche*

**BREAKING AWAY**

Most avalanches occur when melted snow breaks away as large slabs from the rock below. As a slab begins to move, large cracks, called fissures, appear in the snow. These cracks most often appear on bulging slopes and on cornices (slabs of snow that overhang cliff tops).

# Avalanche

ONE OF THE MOST TERRIFYING and dangerous things that can happen in mountainous areas is an avalanche – when huge amounts of snow slide down a mountain slope. A major avalanche can bury buildings – and the people in them. The Swiss Alps, with its numerous ski resorts, is one of the areas most at risk – every year, there are about 10,000 avalanches in that region. Avalanches occur after heavy snowfall has caused snow to build up on mountain slopes. Snow collects in layers – a new one laid during each snowfall. When an avalanche is imminent – when the snow layers are unstable – it can be triggered by strong winds, changes in temperature, or vibrations. Barriers are sometimes built to protect roads or villages, but little can be done to stop the hundreds, or even thousands, of tonnes of snow that tumble down a mountain during a large avalanche. It is important that anybody caught under this cold, heavy blanket is rescued as quickly as possible.

**UNDER COVER**

In areas where avalanches are common, protective sheds are often built over major roads. The sheds allow avalanches to pass over the road. Without these constructions, some roads would be blocked for much of the year.

**BANG, BANG**

When a mass of snow is ready to become an avalanche, it can be set off by the slightest vibration. The best defence against potentially destructive avalanches is to trigger them before too much snow builds up. In places where the threat of serious avalanches is great, patrol teams use explosives to set them off deliberately.

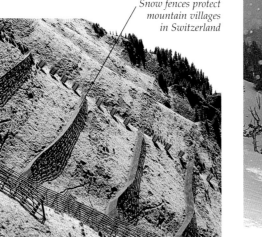

*Snow fences protect mountain villages in Switzerland*

*An avalanche forecaster checks the stability of snow layers*

**SNOW STOPPERS**

Sturdy trees growing on a mountainside can absorb some of the energy of sliding snow. However, logging, acid rain, and increased tourism have dramatically reduced the number of trees in many mountain areas. Artificial barriers made of wood, concrete, or metal, can provide similar protection.

**LOOK CLOSELY**

In regions prone to avalanches it is important to monitor the stability of the snow. Forecasters build snow pits so that they can examine the layers. An avalanche is more likely to occur if any of the layers contains air or is made up of graupel (ice pellets). These pellets can roll over each other allowing large slabs of snow above to break away.

## RIVER OF SNOW

During this massive avalanche on Denali Peak, Alaska, tonnes of powdery, dry snow crashed to the valley floor. Airborne powder avalanches such as this occur soon after a fresh snowfall. They flow like liquid water, throwing up snow in vast splashes on reaching the valley floor. The high-speed mass of snow smothers everything in its path, and compresses the air in front of it creating loud tremors.

*A rescue dog searches for survivors in the Swiss Alps*

## SNIFF SEARCH

Specially trained dogs help to locate people trapped under heavy snow after avalanches. With their highly developed sense of smell, dogs are still more efficient than any electronic sensor. The most famous breed of rescue dog – the Saint Bernard – was named after a saint who, in the 11th century, founded a hospice on an Alpine mountain pass for lost or wounded travellers.

# Floods and landslides

MORE THAN ONE-THIRD of all deaths from natural disasters are caused by flooding. A flash flood occurs when rain is very heavy and rivers break their banks, or sewers quickly become overwhelmed. More widespread devastation is caused by broadscale floods, in which water builds up over a period of weeks. In the Indian subcontinent, seasonal winds called monsoons bring torrential rain every summer. During severe floods, buildings are often ruined and people may drown. When torrential rain combines with high tides and strong winds, those living near a coastline are particularly at risk. Heavy rain can bring another problem – landslides. When large volumes of water mix with soil, the result is a thick liquid that can slip down a hillside, burying anything in its path.

**NOAH'S ARK**
According to the Bible, God was unhappy with the way that humans were treating the world. As a punishment he decided to kill off most of the human race with a flood that would last for 40 days. God chose Noah and his family to survive the deluge. He instructed Noah to build an ark and carry with him a male and female from each of the Earth's species.

Damage caused by the Johnstown flash flood

**DAM BUSTER**
After heavy rain on 31 May 1889, a dam near Johnstown, Pennsylvania, USA, collapsed. Thousands of tonnes of water descended on to the town. The northern part of the city was swept away, and a total of 2,209 people died. The city was left with a huge clear-up operation.

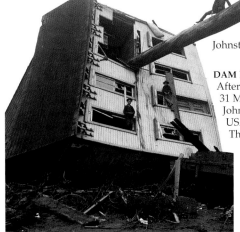

*A farmer in Java frantically tries to save a rice crop from flood-borne volcanic debris*

**DROWNED RICE**
On the island of Java in Indonesia, monsoon rains are usually a blessing. Without these rains, vital rice crops would not survive. But sometimes, particularly heavy rains bring floods that endanger lives and precious crops.

**BREAKING THE BANK**
During the rainy monsoon season, the River Ganges in south Asia frequently bursts its banks. The floods of July and August 1998 were the worst in 20 years and left up to two-thirds of Bangladesh submerged. About 1,500 people died. Some victims drowned, but most died from snakebites or waterborne diseases, because medical assistance was unable to reach them.

**MUDDY RIVER**
Residents of Quindici in Italy fled their homes in May 1998, after two days of torrential rain. As local rivers burst their banks, muddy water poured through the town. The flood left over 3,000 people homeless and killed about 50 people – many of them buried under a thick layer of mud. The clean-up operation took more than three months.

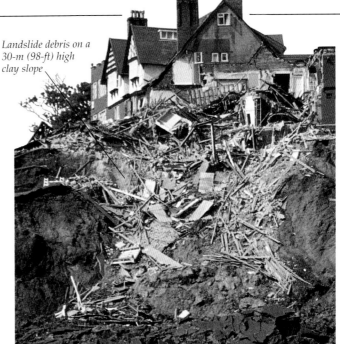

*Landslide debris on a 30-m (98-ft) high clay slope*

**WATERY INTRUDER**
Storm waters broke through the windows of this seaside home in Florida, USA, during Hurricane Andrew in 1991. Hurricanes always bring fierce winds, and a surge of high water produced by the low atmospheric pressure at their centre.

**MOVING MUD**
When water and mud mix on a hillside, gravity pulls the mud and anything else in its path downwards. Part of this hotel in the coastal resort of Scarborough, England, slipped downhill during a landslide in June 1993.

**STORM ON THE WATERFRONT**
These residents of Florida Keys, USA, sought refuge as Hurricane George hit the coastline in 1998. They were forced to battle against 140-kph (90-mph) winds and a surge of water from the Atlantic Ocean. By the time the hurricane reached Florida, severe floods had killed hundreds and affected the lives of thousands of people in the Caribbean.

*Home upturned by a powerful storm surge*

# Deadly droughts

DESERTS ARE PLACES OF PERMANENT DROUGHT. Any region suffering from a lack of water caused by a lower-than-usual rainfall is said to be in drought. As rivers, lakes, and soil dry up, crops fail and animals starve to death. This can lead to widespread famine among humans. Advances in medicine, transport, and communications during the 20th century, have allowed aid agencies to lessen the effects of water scarcity. But as recently as the 1980s, a severe drought claimed many lives in Ethiopia. Although a natural phenomenon, drought is sometimes caused by human activities. In the 1930s, for example, a huge area of the USA became known as the Dust Bowl due to over farming. In times of severe water shortage, efforts have been made to create rain clouds, but with limited success.

**SKIN AND BONES**
Animal carcasses are a common sight during severe droughts. This unfortunate animal dried out before it had a chance to decay.

**POWERFUL PAINTING**
This Australian Aboriginal bark painting comes from Arnhem Land – a hot, dry region of northern Australia. It was used in rain-making ceremonies, and the central image of a stingray symbolizes the "watery" power that summons the rain.

*Animals gather around a waterhole in Namibia, Southern Africa*

**DIMINISHING SUPPLY**
Animals in dry climates often gather around scarce pools of water, called waterholes. In times of drought, more water is lost from the waterhole – from evaporation and drinking – than is supplied by rainfall. There are fewer plants during a drought, too, so food supplies also dwindle. As a result, millions of animals can die during a severe drought.

**WAR AND WANT**
One of the worst droughts of recent times caused a terrible famine in Ethiopia during most of the 1980s. Seasonal droughts are fairly common in Ethiopia, but the civil war that was taking place there made the situation much worse. International aid agencies helped to keep many alive, but the death toll still exceeded 1.5 million people.

**FIGHTING FIRE WITH FIRE**
Forest fires are one disastrous consequence of drought. The dry leaves and wood of dead or dying trees and other plants provide excellent fuel for a raging fire. Most fires start naturally, but sometimes a careless act, such as a dropped match, can cause a forest fire in warm, dry territory. Some trees actually have bark that is fireproof or that peels off when it ignites. There are even trees that will not germinate until their cones are scorched.

## BLOWING IN THE WIND

Most of the world's deserts are covered in sand or sandy soil. Because deserts are in permanent drought, most of the sand is normally dry. The wind can blow dry sand grains around, causing sandstorms that can be uncomfortable, or even dangerous, for people and animals. One result of sandstorms is sand dunes, which make up much of the landscape of the hottest deserts.

## THIRSTY LEAVES

The kokerboom tree is found in the drylands of southwest Africa. It can survive several years of drought, during which time its leaves shrink, having lost most of their moisture.

## BLACK BLIZZARDS

During the 1930s, the Great Plains of the North American Midwest suffered from a long, severe drought. Grasses that usually protected the fields had been ploughed, so when drought struck, the topsoil dried to a dust and was blown away in huge black clouds. Thousands were driven from their homes, and some died of starvation or lung disease caused by inhaling the dust.

## CRACKING UP

Large areas of land with no vegetation can quickly suffer from drought. Plants help to reduce winds that can increase the rate of evaporation from the soil, and they also act as a store of water themselves. Water helps to bind together the grains that make up soil. This is why mud cracks up, becomes brittle, and produces dusty conditions when it is dry.

*Lake Naivasha in Kenya, Africa, dried up by a drought*

# Polar extremes

THE NORTH AND SOUTH POLES are freezing cold all year round. This is because they receive less sunlight than the rest of the world. The area around the north pole, called the Arctic, has no land, only thick ice. Antarctica, around the south pole, has land that is covered by a permanent layer of snow. Winds can be very strong in Antarctica. They are produced as cold air flows off steep slopes into valleys or coastlines. The winds can blow snow into a blizzard that makes it difficult to see. During the long, dark polar winters, temperatures are rarely higher than -40°C (-40°F). The polar regions are much colder than the rest of the world, and play an important part in global weather. Water from the poles, for example, flows towards the equator, as deep, cold currents. These currents affect the weather in many parts of the world.

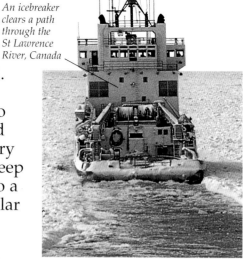

*An icebreaker clears a path through the St Lawrence River, Canada*

**BREAKING THE ICE**
Unlike pure water, salty sea water freezes a few degrees below 0°C (32°F). During winter, when huge amounts of sea ice form, it is important to keep waterways clear. Powerful ice-breaking ships transport vital supplies and also act as research stations.

**ICE STATION**
This research station in Antarctica is the temporary home to scientists from around the world. During the summer, nearly 4,000 people live and work at 42 polar sites. Fewer than 1,000 people live there in winter. By studying the weather at the poles, scientists can gain a more complete picture of the Earth's weather patterns.

**EYE PROTECTION**
Goggles protect eyes from the glare of sunlight, which is reflected by the snow. They also prevent too much heat loss.

**GET A GRIP**
Climbing boots can be specially adapted for icy conditions. A thermal lining helps to retain body heat. Crampons (spikes) can be attached to the soles to provide grip. Trousers can be clipped onto the boots to cover up the ankles.

*Plastic outer layer is tough and durable*

*Spikes help to grip thick, slippery ice*

*Bright red colour makes the jacket stand out in blizzard conditions*

*Elasticated cuffs keep out icy winds*

*Salopettes*

## FLY THE FLAG
The snow that falls or is whipped up during a blizzard can bury important items. Some people plant coloured flags so that they can easily find their tents and supplies when the storm dies down.

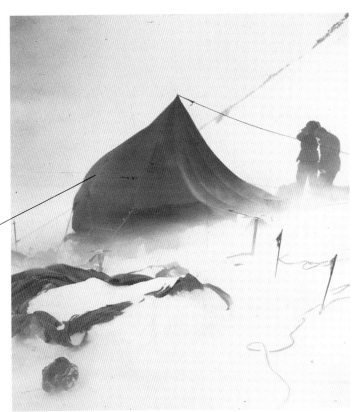

*Pyramid tent designed to withstand high-speed blizzard winds*

## WEATHER STATION
Automatic weather stations are positioned across the polar regions. Forecasting the weather is important for the safety of the scientists who live and work in these hostile environments.

*Weather balloon for gathering data about the atmosphere*

*Undergarment traps a layer of air, which is warmed by the body*

## WEATHER BALLOON
Equipment is loaded into this weather balloon, which will measure the concentration of gases in the Antarctic atmosphere, as well as the temperature high in the air. These measurements can help scientists to test their theories of the weather, and make more accurate forecasts.

*Waterproof nylon outer layer with goosedown stuffing*

*Scientists in Antarctica use a long, hollow drill to extract samples from the sea ice*

## FROZEN IN TIME
Much of the ice at the poles has been frozen for thousands or millions of years. The ice preserves things that were around at the time the ice formed. These include pollens, micro-organisms, dust from volcanoes and comets. By studying samples of melted ice, scientists can discover what the climate was like many years ago.

## STAYING ALIVE
In polar climates, people protect their hands with thick, multi-layered gloves. Hands and feet are most at risk when temperatures fall below freezing. The body shuts off blood to these parts in an attempt to reduce heat loss. But severe conditions can cause frostbite.

## WRAP UP
Polar scientists and explorers wear "extreme cold weather outfits". Outer layers consist of waterproof jacket and salopettes. They are made up of several layers of different materials, which is the best way to reduce heat loss. The most important thing is to cover as much of the body as possible – bare skin loses heat quickly in cold air.

# Weather watch

WHEN A HURRICANE is about to hit, many deaths can be avoided if adequate warning is given. A hurricane can be tracked using weather satellites, but other types of extreme weather, such as drought or a local thunderstorm, are difficult to predict using observations from space. Instead, ground-based measurements – including wind speed, temperature, and atmospheric pressure – are necessary. The data is recorded using a variety of instruments located around the world, on land and at sea. Forecasters use powerful computers to analyze these recordings and to predict a few days in advance how the weather will behave. When bad weather is about to hit, warnings can be issued. The biggest challenges in forecasting are to predict short-lived phenomena such as tornadoes, and long-term conditions such as drought.

**SIGNS FROM SPACE**
Geostationary satellites, such as *Meteostat 4* (left), hover in space about 36,000 km (21,600 miles) above the equator. Day and night, these satellites record atmospheric temperatures and cloud patterns of a particular region.

*Solar cells power the spacecraft*

*About 400 knobbly projections help to stabilize this balloon while in flight*

*Weather instruments are mounted here to give temperature and humidity readings*

*Radar gives a clear picture of clouds and rainfall*

**ROUND RADAR**
Highly sensitive radar equipment enables weather scientists to make increasingly accurate forecasts. The US National Weather Service relies on a network of ground-based Doppler-radar stations to calculate cloud positions, and measure wind speeds and rainfall.

Doppler-radar dome

**HIGH IN THE SKY**
Balloons are an essential part of the world's weather forecasting system. They carry measuring equipment high up into the Earth's atmosphere and transmit readings by radio. This balloon records temperature and humidity. Wind speed can be calculated by using radar to track the balloon in flight. Measurements of conditions in the upper atmosphere are very important for predicting what the weather may do next, and for discovering more about how the weather works.

**WORKING WITH THE WEATHER**
Meteorologists based in research centres around the world use powerful computers to analyze weather measurements taken from land, sea, air, and space. Their findings help them to build a picture of the world's weather patterns. If forecasters predict hurricanes or other extreme weather, they issue warnings, or "watches", via the media.

**FROM FAR AFIELD**
This automatic weather station is located in the middle of a field. It gathers measurements of wind speed and direction, temperature, humidity, and sunlight. Some stations send information to weather satellites, which send the data on to weather agencies. The more data that meteorologists can collect, the better their forecasts will be.

*Instrument for recording wind speed and direction*

*A meteorologist downloads weather data to his portable computer*

**SATELLITE VIEW**
This image was taken by a satellite instrument that is sensitive to infrared radiation. Infrared is heat radiation. It is less energetic than light rays, so is not visible to human eyes, but it can be detected by special cameras. The warmer something is, the more infrared it produces. So, a picture like this can help meteorologists to measure temperature variations across large areas of the world's surface.

**SNOOPING AROUND**
This strange looking aeroplane, nicknamed "Snoopy" because of its long nose, is designed to monitor hurricanes. The plane carries equipment capable of measuring wind strength, speed, and direction. On board the aircraft, a team of meteorologists analyze the recordings.

*Launch of GOES-East aboard a Delta rocket (1981)*

**THERE IT GOES**
GOES (Geostationary Operational Environmental Satellite) monitors the entire Earth's surface (except the regions very close to the poles). The data provided by the latest satellite, GOES-8, enables weather scientists to construct impressive 3-D images of cloud cover.

Weather buoy

**TORNADO PUMP**
Weather forecasts are available across a range of media from newspapers to the Internet. But petrol pumps, such as this one in the US, are perhaps one of the most unlikely sources. A built-in screen displays tornado movements and announces warnings to customers as they re-fuel their vehicles.

**SEA SEARCH**
Buoys, such as this one, carry automatic weather stations. They are left to drift in the sea for weeks, measuring wind speed, temperature, and humidity. The data is then transmitted to research ships. It is important to monitor conditions at sea because the oceans greatly influence the Earth's climate.

# Disaster relief

NATURE CAN CAUSE DESTRUCTION on a huge scale through extreme weather phenomena such as storms, droughts, and floods. When it does, people's lives are dramatically affected, and they need help to keep them alive and well before conditions begin to return to normal. After a hurricane, for example, people may need medical care, or somewhere to stay while their homes are being cleared of floodwater, repaired, or even rebuilt. Food and water supplies may be affected, too. International aid agencies, such as the Red Cross, provide assistance to people who suffer at the hands of the weather. These agencies try to distribute food and medical supplies to wherever they are needed.

*Clean-up operation following a tornado in Connecticut, USA, October 1979*

**UPTURNED LIVES**
A rescuer searches the debris of this upturned home following a tornado in Florida, USA. People who live in southwestern USA have more than their fair share of hurricanes and tornadoes. But however often terrible weather occurs, they can never be fully prepared. Before rebuilding can begin, the inhabitants must be temporarily housed, perhaps in a local school or supermarket.

**DAMAGE DEMOLITION**
The building above was completely destroyed by a powerful tornado. Before it can be rebuilt, it needs to be completely demolished, with the help of this powerful digger. The governments of wealthy countries set aside emergency funds with which to pay for rebuilding work. Poorer countries must often rely on outside aid.

**PORTABLE WATER**
Even during a flood, fresh drinking water is often in short supply. This Filipino boy is collecting fresh water from a tank, because his water supply was cut off by flood damage.

*Temporary water tank provides fresh water to flood victims*

**MOPPING UP**
One of the main priorities in an area hit by flooding is to drain off the excess water. Emergency services use powerful pumps to clear the streets. Sandbags protect properties from floodwater, and also control the direction of the flow.

## AIR MEALS

When any kind of natural disaster strikes a remote location, the quickest way to bring aid to the area is to drop supplies from the sky. The food carried by this aeroplane helped many people stay alive during a severe drought in Sudan, Africa. Each of the tightly bound parcels contained mostly flour, oil, and canned fruit. It is difficult to drop water in these parcels, even though it is often what is most needed.

*Makeshift shelters in a refugee camp in Ethiopia*

## TEMPORARY HOMES

When drought brought famine to Ethiopia in 1989, the United Nations set up this camp in Sidamo Province. Forty-five thousand people took refuge from the famine here. Each family was given some plastic sheeting to act as a temporary shelter, a sleeping mat, and cooking utensils, as well as food and water. Refugees had to find their own materials for cooking and for building huts, putting a great strain on scarce resources.

*Emergency food supplies*

## DISEASE PREVENTION

Epidemics can break out rapidly in disaster sites, and are a common cause of death. This aid worker is spraying insecticide to kill off disease-spreading mosquitoes, which thrive in murky floodwaters. Care must be taken to use insecticides that will not harm people when they filter into the water supply.

## ALL DRIED UP

When this picture was taken, there had been no rain in the Suguta Valley, Kenya, for seven years. Famine is common during a serious drought, particularly in remote areas where it is difficult to obtain supplies. This is why food aid is important. Here, the food is being supplied by Oxfam, a charity that was set up to help fight against famine.

# Nature's survivors

THE WORLD'S PLANTS AND ANIMALS are all well suited to their environments. If they were not, they would soon die out, particularly in extreme climates such as deserts. The plants and animals that live today are different from those of long ago. Some living things are so well adapted to their surroundings, in such strange ways, that you may think that they have been specially designed to live there. But living things adapt to their surroundings gradually – over many generations. Camels, for example, have developed the ability to overcome the scarcity of water in the desert. In dry places, plants retain as much water as they can. In rainy places, they are actually able to stop too much water from collecting on their leaves.

**FEATHER COAT**
Snowy owls live in Arctic regions. Their soft, fluffy feathers hold lots of air, which insulates their bodies against the harsh cold. Snowy owls even have feathers around their claws. If the weather becomes hot, these owls cannot take off their winter coats. They cool themselves by spreading their wings and panting.

**FAT MONSTER**
The gila monster is a lizard that lives in Mexico and the southwestern US. During the warm, rainy season, food – in the form of eggs, baby birds, and rodents – is plentiful, and the gila monster eats well. During this time, it stores body fat, on which it can live for long periods during the cold, dry winter.

*Fat stored in the tail provides energy during the winter*

**UPSIDE-DOWN TREE**
The strange-looking baobab tree is described in a myth. The story explains how the tree angered the gods by complaining. The gods punished the tree by uprooting it and re-planting it upside down. The real reason for the tree's odd appearance is that it only has leaves for up to three months per year. This, together with the tree's store of water in its huge trunk, help to enable the tree to survive the dry season in its native East Africa.

*Drip tip of a rainforest leaf*

**USEFUL TIPS**
In a rainforest, it is not unusual for about 1 m (3 ft) of rain to fall each month during the rainy season. Plants depend on water to survive, but if their leaves were constantly coated with a layer of water, they would die. So, some rainforest leaves have developed pointed "drip tips", to carry the water away.

**STEMMING THE FLOW**
A plant's leaves are covered with tiny holes, called stomata, that allow water to escape. As water evaporates through the stomata, more is drawn up through the plant from the soil. Where water is scarce, such as in the desert, plants usually have fewer or smaller leaves. Many cacti, such as this hedgehog cactus, have no leaves at all. These plants are just large water-holding stems.

**SOME LIKE IT WET**
Red-eyed tree frogs are well adapted to life in the rainforest. They have suckers on their feet that help them to clamber among the branches. Like all frogs, tree frogs have moist skin. If their skin dries out, they will die. So, far from being under threat from the heavy rainfall in the rainforest, tree frogs thrive in their damp environment.

**UNDERGROUND MOVEMENT**
Most amphibians have a slimy skin, which must remain moist at all times. During times of drought, many amphibians remain in burrows or gather together in a moist location, such as a rotting log. In countries with a dry season, some frogs become totally dormant when water supplies are low, surrounding themselves in a moist mud cocoon.

Australian burrowing frog

**WATER FACTORY**
Like many other animals that live in the constant drought of the desert, the camel can actually make water from its own body fat. A camel can use a quarter of its body weight to stay alive, without suffering any ill effects.

*A camel can drink the equivalent of a bath full of water in just a few minutes*

**IN A COLD CLIMATE**
One of the few animals to live in the harsh conditions of the Antarctic all year round is the Emperor penguin. With waterproof feathers and thick fat layers under the skin, the penguins are perfectly adapted for survival on land and in the icy seas. When penguins are tending their eggs and young, they are unable to swim off in search of food. At these times, their body fat provides an essential source of energy.

*Overlapping feathers are closely packed to keep out fierce winds*

*Fluffy-feathered chicks huddle together for warmth*

*Feet are small to minimize heat loss*

# Climate change

THE CLIMATE OF A PARTICULAR REGION is the typical weather in that area over the last 30 years. But climates can change. There are, for example, several known periods in history when temperatures across the world were much lower than they are now. During these "ice ages", more of the oceans' water froze, and the polar ice-caps grew larger. Ice also covered more land, in the form of huge glaciers. One of the causes of ice ages is the variation in the distance between the Earth and the sun. Some scientists believe that huge meteorite impacts are also sometimes to blame. At other times in the Earth's history, higher than normal temperatures have wiped out civilizations. Scientists use many techniques, including examining fossils or tree rings, to "read" climate records.

**EVER-CHANGING SEA**
The ammonoid, or ammonite, was a shelled marine animal that lived in warm oceans until about 66 million years ago. But ammonoid fossils have been found in the rocks under the oceans of Antarctica. Because Antarctica was not always at the south pole, it was not always cold. Like all continents, Antarctica has drifted thousands of kilometres over millions of years.

Frost fair on the Thames River in London, 1813

**LOST CIVILIZATION**
Dramatic changes in the climate can force people to move from their homes, and can even cause the end of civilizations. The Anasazi civilization lived in these caves, in the southwest of what is now the USA, until about 1280. They were forced to move away by a drought that lasted for about 23 years.

**MINI ICE AGE**
Between about 1500 and 1850, much of Europe experienced what is referred to as the "Little Ice Age". The average temperature was only a few degrees lower than normal, but this was enough to freeze huge amounts of sea water. Winters were very harsh, and rivers often froze over.

*Thick, woolly coat provides insulation*

*Huge curved ivory tusks were used to ward off predators, and probably to sweep aside snow when feeding on grassy plains*

**COLD-CLIMATE ELEPHANT**
During the last Great Ice Age, woolly mammoths lived in the icy tundra regions of North America, Europe, and Asia. Mammoths died out about 10,000 years ago, as the world's climate began to warm up.

*Hair-covered trunk to keep out the cold*

## TREE CIRCLES

Trees grow thicker with each year they are alive. New living wood is created in a layer beneath the bark. Each year's growth appears as a ring. The warmer the climate is in a particular year, the more growth that occurs, and the thicker the ring becomes. By analyzing the width of tree rings, scientists can calculate the average temperatures for each year of the tree's life.

*The thicker a tree ring, the warmer the climate in that year*

*Bristlecone pines growing on the White Mountains, California, USA*

## LIVING CLIMATE RECORD

The oldest living trees are bristlecone pines found in California and Nevada, USA. Some of these trees are over 4,000 years old, and are a living record of the history of the climate. The tree rings can be analyzed by boring into the trunk and removing a long thin sample of wood.

## SPACE DUST

This crater, in what is now Arizona, USA, records the impact of a huge meteorite that hit the Earth 50,000 years ago. Millions of tonnes of dust were thrown up into the air, and most of it stayed in the air for about a year. The dust reflected much of the sun's light back into space. Some scientists believe that the dust from meteor impacts can cause reduced global temperatures.

## MELTING FUTURE?

The world's average temperature is rising slowly – this is called global warming. Some scientists blame human activity, such as the burning of fuels, for some of this temperature increase. If global warming continues at its present rate, more and more of the ice at the north and south poles will melt causing flooding in many parts of the world during the next century.

*A massive iceberg in Greenland dwarfs a passing fishing trawler*

# El Niño phenomenon

EVERY TWO TO TEN YEARS, part of the Pacific Ocean, near to the coast of South America, becomes warmer during winter than normal. Pacific winds change direction, blowing warm water eastwards towards South America. This phenomenon – known as El Niño – causes extreme weather throughout the tropics, and can last up to four years. Countries as far apart as Australia and Africa may suffer disruption to their normal rainfall patterns, which can result in severe flooding or drought. El Niño can also affect weather further afield than the tropics. It can cause average winter temperatures over North America to fall, and can increase winter rainfall over northwestern Europe. As El Niño can be predicted several months ahead, meteorologists are able to issue early warnings. These can allow farmers to alter their crops to suit the forecast conditions.

**HOT AND COLD**
This map of the Earth has been put together using information from satellites. It shows how the temperatures across the world were affected during an El Niño in 1983. The orange and red areas show warmer than normal temperatures, the blue areas are cooler than normal. The large red and orange patch over the eastern Pacific Ocean is due to El Niño.

**HARD TIMES**
El Niño (Spanish for "the Christ child") was given its name by Peruvian fishermen, because it appears around Christmas time. When El Niño winds blow warm water over the cool Peruvian seas, large numbers of fish disappear. This is because the plankton on which the fish feed cannot grow in warmer waters. Many Peruvians, whose livelihoods and survival depend on fishing, also suffer terribly at the hands of El Niño.

**ON THE ROCKS**
Sea lions and seabirds off the western coast of South America often die from starvation during an El Niño. They depend on the fish that thrive on the plankton in the normally cool waters. When El Niño hits, the cooler waters are pushed downwards, and the fish swim deeper – out of reach of the sea lions and seabirds.

**WARM AND WET**
During the 1998 El Niño, floods in Kenya, Africa, ruined maize crops, and spread diseases such as malaria. Kenya normally has low rainfall, but during an El Niño, warmer water mixes with the waters off the Kenyan coast. The subsequent increase in rainfall often causes flooding.

**HEAVY SNOW**
Changes in currents in the Pacific Ocean during an El Niño often affect the west coast of the USA. While some areas suffer from floods, other parts become much colder. For example, the El Niño of 1997–1998 brought much higher than normal snow levels to the mountains of southern California, USA.

## SEABED SKELETONS
Bleached coral is a reliable indicator of the presence of an El Niño. Tiny colourful plants, called algae, live on coral, and are vital to its survival. They move away when the sea's temperature rises, leaving behind the coral's white "skeleton". In areas where temperatures are higher than normal, rich coral reefs become pale and barren as they die.

## BURNING UP
In 1998, El Niño brought drought to Sumatra, Indonesia. The drought had made the trees very dry and forest fires burned out of control. The fires burned for weeks, and covered Sumatra with thick smoke. It became so dark that drivers had to use their headlights during the day.

## DROUGHT ALERT
El Niño reduces rainfall in Brazil, which sometimes leads to drought. During the El Niño of 1987, Brazil's grain production fell by 80 per cent. In 1992, however, scientists were able to predict the onset of El Niño. Farmers planted crops that would survive a drought, and the resulting harvest was only slightly less than normal.

## ALL DRIED UP
During an El Niño, winds push warm water eastwards towards South America, and away from Australia in the west. The cooler waters around eastern Australia lead to reduced rainfall, and large areas suffer from drought. During 1997, warnings of the approaching El Niño caused many Australian farmers to abandon their land.

## WASHED AWAY
Much of the west coast of Peru and Chile, in South America, is very dry, because the coastal waters there are normally cool. During an El Niño in February 1998, however, rain began to fall at an incredible rate – up to 15 cm (6 in) every day. The floods that resulted broke river banks, and in some cases swept away whole villages.

# Freaky conditions

THE EARTH'S ATMOSPHERE, together with the sun, provides all the weather conditions experienced on Earth. For example, the sun's energy evaporates water into the atmosphere, to produce clouds. Most people experience sunshine, wind, rain, and perhaps snow at some time, but the sun and the atmosphere can also create strange conditions. Many people have seen a rainbow, caused by sunlight hitting raindrops and bouncing back; but few have seen a moonbow. Other tricks of light include haloes, mirages, and the spooky Brocken Spectre. Electricity in thunderclouds can also produce strange effects other than lightning, such as St Elmo's Fire. Electric charge is also responsible for the beautiful aurora lights. Some of the world's rarest and most strange phenomena remain unexplained.

**MYSTERIOUS GLOW**
One eerie effect of an electrified thundercloud is St Elmo's Fire. This is a rare bluish-green light that glows at the tips of pointed objects, such as a ship's rigging, during a storm. An object may glow in this way as it slowly leaks an electric charge that is in turn attracted to the charge at the base of a thundercloud.

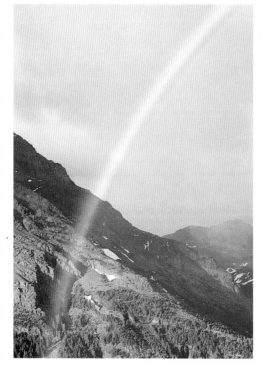

**COLOURS IN THE SKY**
When the sun is fairly low in the sky behind you, and it is raining, you may see a rainbow. Light from the sun reflects off the inside surfaces of raindrops, and bends as it travels through them. Each of the colours that make up sunlight is bent to a different angle, which is why a rainbow appears as a band of colours.

**A GHOSTLY SIGHT**
Sometimes, climbers on high mountains see huge human figures before them. This effect is called the Brocken Spectre, after the Brocken peak in Germany, where the phenomenon has been most famously reported. The figures are simply the climbers' own shadows cast on the bases of nearby clouds. Sometimes, the shadows are surrounded by colourful haloes called Brocken Bows.

**GLOWING GLOBES**
Thousands of people worldwide have reported seeing balls of light that either hover in midair or drift along before exploding violently or fading away. This effect, called ball lightning, is most likely an electrical phenomenon caused by thunderstorms.

**COLOURS AT MOONRISE**
Just after the rising of a bright full moon in the east, shortly after the sun sets in the west, you may be lucky enough to see a moonbow. This is formed in the same way as a normal rainbow, so you must have the moon behind you and it must also be raining in the west. Moonbows are very rare.

*As the hollow cylinder of snow moves it gathers more snow on the outside*

**MAGICAL SNOWBALLS**
Snow sometimes plays a clever trick by rolling itself up just like a sleeping bag. This only happens when new snow falls on old and is blown by a strong warm wind. Although it is rare to see them forming, on a good day you may find a whole field full of spontaneous snowballs.

*Rock reflected in the sand gives the illusion of water*

**DISTORTED VIEW**
Reports of shimmering reflections in the desert and ships hanging upside down above the horizon at sea have been recorded for centuries. These are not pure fantasy, but refer to mirages, which are produced when light from distant objects bends as it passes through air at different temperatures.

## SUN HALO

When sunlight passes through cirrus, or high-altitude clouds, a halo can be seen around the sun. Since ancient times, some people have believed haloes are a sign of imminent rain. This is one piece of weather folklore that has some truth to it – the presence of cirrus clouds does often precede rainfall.

## SUNSET SPARK

Occasionally, on clear days, just as the sun is setting or rising, a mysterious green flash lights up the sky. This effect is only visible over a definite horizon, such as the one at sea. The flashes are caused by sunlight being bent and scattered by dust particles in the atmosphere.

## AURORAS

Spectacular displays of coloured light called auroras can often be seen near the Earth's north and south poles, and sometimes from farther afield. The light is produced high in the atmosphere as electrically charged solar particles are attracted towards the magnetic poles, and collide with air molecules.

# Weather beyond Earth

THE SUN IS A STAR that sits at the centre of our solar system, and is orbited by nine planets and their moons. The sun's radiation causes weather on Earth by heating the atmosphere. Without an atmosphere, a planet can have no wind, rain, or snow. Mercury and many of the planets' moons – including Earth's moon – have virtually no atmosphere at all. The planets Venus and Mars do have atmospheres, and some of their weather is similar to Earth. Both planets have clouds and extreme winds, for example. Beyond Mars are the "gas giants" – Jupiter, Saturn, Uranus, and Neptune – which are huge balls of gas, with a small liquid or rocky core. The gases that make up these planets swirl around as the planets spin, forming spiral storms similar to hurricanes on Earth. Further from the sun than the gas giants is the tiny planet Pluto, where it is too cold for an atmosphere to form.

**BLUE NEPTUNE**
Neptune's winds blow as fast as 2,500 kph (1,575 mph), and are the strongest winds in the solar system. The planet appears blue because the atmosphere contains methane gas. The white cloud bands (above) are probably made of frozen methane, which cools as it rises.

*The sky on Mars is pink during the day*

*The sun is more than 100 times larger than Earth*

**DUST STORM**
Mars is covered by a layer of dust that contains iron oxide – a compound in rust – which gives the planet its reddish colour. Although the atmosphere on Mars is much thinner than on Earth, Mars does have fierce winds that blow huge amounts of dust across the planet's surface.

**VENUSIAN VOLCANOES**
The surface of Venus has many features that are similar to those found on Earth. There are volcanoes, for example, although most have been inactive for millions of years. Like the volcanoes on Earth, when those on Venus erupted they contributed gases to the atmosphere, which play a part in the planet's weather.

## RUNNING RINGS
You can identify the planet Saturn – the second largest in the solar system – by its prominent rings. Like all the gas giants, Saturn is nearly all atmosphere, and becomes more and more dense the further towards the centre you go. The planet is warmed by the sun, but in some places, the outer atmosphere is still a chilly -190°C (-310°F).

*Superbolt lightning storm*

*High-powered winds of up to 1,800 kph (1,118 mph) encircle Saturn*

## SCORCHING STORM
The sun is a ball of extremely hot gas. The surface is much cooler than the centre, but at more than 5,000°C (10,000°F), it is still hot enough to vaporize diamonds. The surface is a turbulent place, too. Huge storms, called prominences, caused by the sun's strong magnetic field, throw millions of tonnes of searing hot gas into space.

*Storm prominence erupts on the sun*

Ultraviolet image of the sun

## SPINNING SPOTS
Jupiter – the largest of all the planets – spins rapidly. It takes less than ten hours to make one rotation. This movement causes the planet's atmosphere to swirl around, and is responsible for the Great Red Spot (above). This spot is a storm similar to a hurricane, but about twice the size of Earth. Jupiter's great storm has been raging for at least 330 years, since it was first observed.

*Sulphuric cloud bands*

*Europa's icy surface*

## CHARGED UP
Lightning on Earth is caused by updraughts of air in huge thunderclouds. Other planets have lightning, too, produced in the same way. Jupiter has particularly energetic lightning storms at its magnetic poles, which is thought to be caused partly by the planet's strong magnetic field.

## ICY EUROPA
One of Jupiter's moons, Europa, has a thin atmosphere made up largely of oxygen. It is a rocky ball coated in a layer of smooth water ice, which appears to be similar to pack-ice on Earth. Some space scientists think that there may be liquid water beneath the ice. If this is true then there could be some form of life in Europa's seas.

## MOLTEN VENUS
With a surface temperature hot enough to melt lead, Venus is the hottest planet in the solar system. The planet is shrouded in thick clouds of sulphuric acid, and the atmospheric pressure at its surface is 90 times higher than that on Earth.

# Index

# Acknowledgments

**Dorling Kindersley would like to thank:**

Sheila Collins for design assistance.

**Indexer:** Chris Bernstein

**Illustrators:** Eric Thomas and John Woodcock

**Photographers:** Peter Anderson, Jeoff Brightling, Jane Burton, Peter Chadwick, Andy Crawford, Geoff Dann, Mike Dunning, Steve Gorton, Frank Greenaway, Ellen Howden, Colin Keates, Dave King, Andrew Nelmerm, Janet Peckham, Kim Sayer, Karl Shone, Andreas Von Einsiedel, Jerry Young, and Michel Zabé

**Picture credits**
The publisher would like to thank the following for their kind permission to reproduce their photographs:

t=top, b=below, l=left, r=right, c=centre:

**Alison Anholt White:** 16c.
**Ardea London Ltd:** Francois Gohier 12bl; M. Watson 39bl.
**Associated Press Ap:** 37tl, 41tl, 41b; SLF Jennings 30-31; Topham 48tr.
**Bridgeman Art Library, London / New York:** Thor's fight with the Giants, 1872 by Winge, Marten Eskil 1825-96, Nationalmuseum, Stockholm, Sweden; Plato and Aristotle, detail of the School of Athens, 1510-1511 (fresco), Vatican Museum and Galleries 8bc.
**British Museum, London:** 9ca, 9cr.
**Bruce Coleman Ltd:** Jules Cowan; 53tr Jeff Foott 4b, 16-17; Johnny Johnson 51bc; Allan G.

Potts 54-55b.
**Corbis UK Ltd:** 39r, 39r; Bettmann 10cr, 24crb, 40cl, 43c; Lowell Georgia 6tr, 38tl; David Muench 52cl; Galen Rowell 39cr.
**Sylvia Cordaiy Photo Library Ltd:** Nigel Rolstone 24-25b.
**Ecoscene:** Nick Hawkes 38bl.
**Environmental Images:** John Arnold 45cr.
**E.T. Archive:** Guildhall Library 52cr.
**Mary Evans Picture Library:** 24bc, 28cl.
**Glasgow Museums, The Burrell Collection:** 42tl.
**Ronald Grant Archive:** WB & Universal 22-23cl.
**Robert Harding Picture Library:** 13cl, 13b, 34-35a; Jon Gardley 45tr; Dr. A.C. Waltham 34-35b.
**Hulton Getty:** Fox 34cr; Tony Waltham 41tr; G. Williams Photos 36tr; Keystone 32cl; Painted by Stephen Pearce, engraved by John Scott 16tl.
**Hutchison Library:** 33r.
**ICRC:** Clive Shirley 49bl.
**INAH:** Mexican Museum Authority, Michael Zabe 9bl.
**Kristen Klaver:** 47clb, 47bl.
**FLPA – Images of nature:** 30-31ca; J.C. Allen 26bl; D. Hoadley 22-23c; H. Hoflinger 20cr; NRC 27cl; R. Jennings 56c; S. Jonasson 15br.
**Magnum:** Bruce Davidson 17ca; Steve McCurry 40bl.
**Gene Moore:** 26-27, 27tl, 27cr.
**N.A.S.A.:** 4tr, 4c, 6cl, 4cl, 28-29, 47br, 58tr, 58-59c, 58b, 59c, 59bl, 59br, 59t; 6bc, 18cl.
**National Maritime Museum, London:** 10cr.
**Courtesy of the National Science Foundation:** 45tl, 45cla.
**NHPA:** A.N.T. 21cr.
**NOAA:** Dennis J. Sigrist, International Tsunami Information Centre, Honolulu, Hawaii 34bl.

**Novosti:** A. Varfolomeyer 26tr.
**Oxford Scientific Films:** Daniel J. Cox 44cl; Warren Faidley 6bl, 19br, 25a, 28tl; Michael Fogden 42c; Richard Henman 54bl; Mantis Wildlife Films 51cr; Colin Monteath, Hegehog House 32b; Ian West 22-23clb; Stan Osolinksi 56cl; Stouffer Enterprises Inc./Animals Animals 14b.
**Panos Pictures:** Trygue Bolstad 43tl; Heidi Bradner 13tr; Jerry Callow 8cl; Neil Cooper 43cb; Jeremy Hartley 42tr, 58cl; Sim Holmes 4tc, 28bl; Zed Nelson 28tr; Clive Shirley 54c, 55bc; © Tatlow 55tr.
**PA News Photo Library:** EPA/Pool 16tr.
**Pitt Rivers Museum, Oxford:** 9cra.
**Planet Earth Pictures:** Georgette Douwma 55tl; Jiri Lochman 55cr.
**John E. Purchase:** 56bl.
**Rex Features:** 16cl, 31tr, 40br, 41cl, 48bl; Jean Yves Desfoux 36cl; Sipa Press 20-21.
**Courtesy Of The Rosenberg Library, Galveston, Texas:** 30bl.
**Royal British Columbia Museum:** 52bl.
**Scala:** Museo della Scienza Firenze 4tl, 6br, 10br, 10l, 11bl; S. Maria Novella (farmacia), Firenze 11c.
**Science Photo Library:** Eric Bernard, Jerrican 36bl; Jean-Loup Charmet 24c; Jim Goodwin 48cl; Ben Johnson 34cl; Damien Lovegrove 56crb; Pete Menzel 24cl NASA. 25bc; NASA GSFC 54tr; Claude Nuridsany & Marie Perennesu 5tl, 36cr; David Parker 46bl, 47tr, 53cl; Pekka Parviainen 57clb; Fred K. Smith 5bc, 18tr.
**Still Pictures:** Adrian Arbib 49br; Nigel Dickenson 48br; Filho-UNEP 55c; G. Grifiths/Christian Aid 54clb; Olivier Langrand 50cb; Andre Maslennikor 42bc; Gil Moti 32cr; Hartmut

Schwarzbach 42br, 49tr; Hjalte Tin 49cl; UNEP. 57.
**Courtesy of Jeff Piotrowski/ Storm Productions Inc. USA:** 6cr, 20cl, 20clb, 20bl, 22-23tr, 22-23br.
**Tony Stone Images:** 52-53b; Vince Streano 31crb.
**Stock Shot:** Gary Pearl 38cb; Peter Quenault 38tr; Jess Stock 13tl, 38cl.
**Sygma:** 31cra, 31br; Paul/Pierre Pollin 37b; Claude Poulet 44tr.
**Topham Picturepoint:** 22-23r.
**Travel Ink:** David Toase 34tr.
**Weatherstock:** Warren Faidley 6tl, 7tr, 12tr, 13cr, 37tr, 46bc, 47tl, 57cl, 59cr.

**Jacket:**
**Associated Press Ap:** SLF Jennings back br.
**E.T. Archive:** National Library Mexico back tr.
**Mary Evans Picture Library:** front bl, inside flap cr.
**Image Bank:** back tl, front tl.
**Magnum:** Steve McCurry inside flap br.
**Gene Moore:** front clb.
**N.A.S.A.:** front br
**N.H.P.A.:** A.N.T. front cl.
**Oxford Scientific Films:** Warren Faidley back cla, inside flap bl.
**Panos Pictures:** Sim Holmes inside flap bc; Zed Nelson back crb.
**Jeff Piotrowski/Storm Productions:** front cla.
**Science Photo Library:** Fred K. Smith inside flap tl; NASA/Goodard Space Flight Centre back cl; Pete Menzel back clb; SLF Jennings back cr.
**The Stock Market:** front c.
**Sygma:** back bl.
**Weatherstock:** front cra, back cra, back tcr, inside flap tr, spine.

# DK EYEWITNESS GUIDES

# SUBJECTS

## HISTORY

AFRICA

ARMS & ARMOUR

BATTLE

CASTLE

CHINA

COWBOY

EXPLORER

KNIGHT

MEDIEVAL LIFE

MYTHOLOGY

NORTH AMERICAN INDIAN

PIRATE

PRESIDENTS

RUSSIA

SHIPWRECK

TITANIC

VIKING

WITCH & WIZARD

## ANCIENT WORLDS

ANCIENT EGYPT

ANCIENT GREECE

ANCIENT ROME

AZTEC

BIBLE LANDS

MUMMY

PYRAMID

## THE BEGINNINGS OF LIFE

ARCHAEOLOGY

DINOSAUR

EARLY PEOPLE

PREHISTORIC LIFE

## THE ARTS

CINEMA

COSTUME

DANCE

MUSIC

WRITING

## TECHNOLOGY

BOAT

CAR

FLYING MACHINE

FUTURE

INVENTION

SPACE EXPLORATION

TRAIN

## PAINTING

GOYA

IMPRESSIONISM

LEONARDO

MANET

MONET

PERSPECTIVE

RENAISSANCE

VAN GOGH

WATERCOLOUR

## SCIENCE
ASTRONOMY
CHEMISTRY
EARTH
ECOLOGY
ELECTRICITY
ELECTRONICS
ENERGY
EVOLUTION
FORCE & MOTION
HUMAN BODY
LIFE
LIGHT
MATTER
MEDICINE
SKELETON
TECHNOLOGY
TIME & SPACE

## SPORT
AMERICAN FOOTBALL
BASEBALL
FOOTBALL
OLYMPICS
SPORT

## ANIMALS
AMPHIBIAN
BIRD
BUTTERFLY & MOTH
CAT
DOG
EAGLE
ELEPHANT
FISH
GORILLA
HORSE
INSECT
MAMMAL
REPTILE
SHARK
WHALE

## HABITATS
ARCTIC & ANTARCTIC
DESERT
JUNGLE
OCEAN
POND & RIVER
SEASHORE

## THE EARTH
CRYSTAL & GEM
FOSSIL
HURRICANE & TORNADO
PLANT
ROCK & MINERAL
SHELL
TREE
VOLCANO
WEATHER

## THE WORLD AROUND US
BUILDING
CRIME & DETECTION
FARM
FLAG
MEDIA
MONEY
RELIGION
SPY

Future updates and editions will be available online at www.dk.com

# A–Z

# DK EYEWITNESS GUIDES

# 1–110

Future updates and editions will be available online at www.dk.com

# DK EYEWITNESS GUIDES

# 1–110

Future updates and editions will be available online at www.dk.com